What They Didn't Teach You in **French** Class

What They Didn't Teach You in **French** Class

Slang phrases for the café, club, bar, bedroom, ball game and more

Adrien Clautrier and Henry Rowe

 ULYSSES PRESS

Published by:
Ulysses Press
P.O. Box 3440
Berkeley, CA 94703
www.ulyssespress.com

ISBN: 978-1-64604-393-4 (paperback)
ISBN: 978-1-61243-682-1 (hardback)
Library of Congress Control Number: 2016957693

Printed in the United States
10 9 8 7 6 5 4 3 2 1

Managing editor: Claire Chun
Editors: Shayna Keyles, Alice Riegert
Proofreader: Lauren Harrison
Design and illustrations: what!design @ whatweb.com
Production: Yesenia Garcia-Lopez

This book is dedicated to Eric and to the soccer club ASPEN/St. Cloud.

Table of Contents

Using This Book

In high school, you learned that France is home to the "Mona Lisa" and the Eiffel Tower. Your online language program taught you that there's possibly no such thing as a regular verb in French and way too many words have more vowels than consonants. And maybe you were even lucky enough to study abroad and have a restaurant confront you with those baffling crossover *escargot* tongs and the goose liver *foie gras*, which California banned because it's made by force-feeding corn down the throat of a goose.

But Mrs. Fournier's class didn't teach you how to navigate a hookup via text message, and it didn't give you ammunition to answer when exchange student Bernard calls you a *connard* at rugby practice.

So here's *What They Didn't Teach You in French Class*. (You're welcome!) In this updated version of *Dirty French*, you'll find all your answers conveniently arranged by theme to handle just about every situation you'll encounter. This book won't cure your hangover and it won't cover unexplained charges on your credit card, but it will teach you how to order a round for new-found friends, how to sound like a local in the South of France, and how to handle yourself out on the town. You'll even know how to tell Jean-Pierre to put on a condom or get the hell out!

But a few words are in order before we jump in.

At times this book gets a bit nasty. Not Comedy Central or *SNL* dirty, with bleeps and stars—this stuff is Jim Jefferies nasty, Amy Schumer raunchy. It's important to remember that slang is highly situational: the wrong word can escalate a confrontation very quickly, or end a budding friendship. So use these expressions only with people your own age, in contexts where you know what's going on.

Also, if your entire contact with French is a community college class you dropped after three days, you'll have a hard time doing much with this book. As the title suggests, *What They Didn't Teach You in French Class* was written with the assumption that you already know enough French to get by. After all, this is a slang book, and learning slang tends to come after mastering how to make great philosophical affirmations like "I live in an apartment" and "Yes, my dog has four legs." So, this isn't a beginner's grammar book. This is a book designed to take your French to the next level.

Except in special cases, the English is given first, followed by the French. Sometimes the French is given with alternatives—*laid(e)*, *mon/ma*—to account for gender differences. As we said before, this isn't a grammar book and you're not an idiot, so we expect that you'll be able to figure it out without any more explanation than that.

Pronouncing French

Here's a brief refresher on pronunciation. This is not how to name the letters of the alphabet, but how to pronounce them when they appear in words.

A, à = ah
B = bay
C = kah (before "a, o, u"), say (before "e, i")
Ç = say
D = day
E, è = euh (like the second "e" in "telephone")
É = ay
F = eff
G = gg (before "a, o, u"), zhee (before "e, i")
H = [silent]
I = ee
J = zhay
K = kah

L = elle

M = emm

N = enn

O, ô = oh

P = pay

Q = keww

R = airr

S = esse

T = tay

U = eww (shape your mouth like a chicken's bunghole—*un cul de poule*—and you'll say it right)

V = vay

X = eeks

Y = ee

Z = z

Je = zheuh (like the "ge" in "garage")

Tu = tew

Il, ils = eel (they're pronounced exactly the same; context is what lets people know when it's plural)

Elle, elles = elle (you might want to check the explanation right above)

On = ohhhn

Nous = nou

Vous = vou (like "voodoo")

The hardest thing for Americans to pronounce is the vowels. That's because we Americans flatline our sentences in monotones, and aren't used to pronouncing words with sharp emphasis. To really tap into proper French pronunciation, an easy way is to imitate the old Inspecteur Clouseau and speak with an ouuuuut-raaay-juss Freeeench ack-cent: "Hey dude, ya wanna go get high?" would become "hAAY dewwwd, yoooo waaahn toooo geeet hIII?" Don't worry, you'll get the hang of it.

CHAPTER 1

Meet & Greet
Amabilités

....

Hello
Bonjour

You probably shouldn't use French slang with strangers, especially if they're over 30, unless you want to get on their nerves right away. So when in doubt stick with the classic *Bonjour*. After you get to know someone a little better, feel free to use some of these slangier expressions. (As for women, you'll get all kinds of attention if you try these with people you don't know.)

Hi
Salut

Hey!
Ho!

Hey, you; Hey, baby
Coucou

Yo, guys!
Oh, les gars!

Yo, girls!
Oh, les filles!; Salut, les girls!

Greetings are a bit different on the telephone.

Hello?
Âllo?

Hey!
Salut!

Good morning
Bonjour

In French, there are a bunch of informal variations on "good morning" and "good evening" for you to choose from.

Mornin', honey!
*Bonjour, **mon chéri/ma chérie**!*

Hey, babe, good morning!
Bonjour, toi!

Mornin'!
'Jour!

Evenin'!
'Soir!

Night!
Bonne nuit!

The hello kiss
La bise

You probably know that the French greet each other with little pecks on the cheek, like pigeons doing a mating dance. This is the local equivalent of the American "college hug" (which the French think is weird—they'll feel like you're coming on to them if you even try it).

Women exchange these kisses with all friends, male and female, when seeing them for the first time each day. If you kiss one person in a group, you should kiss them all (as long as they're roughly your age). And just go cheek to cheek and smooch the air; don't actually touch your lips to them.

Things are a bit different for men, who only use this kiss to greet female friends and their family. Among male friends, they simply shake hands.

Let's shake.
On se serre la main.

How 'bout a hug?
On s'embrasse?

Here's a kiss hello.
Je te fais la bise.

Kisses!
Bisous!; Bises!
This is what you might say on the phone or at the end of a message.

Kiss me on the mouth.
Embrasse-moi sur la bouche.

Gimme a big kiss.
Tire-moi un patin/une galoche.
The origins of the expressions aren't known for sure, but *un patin* is a skate, so it probably means "to slide in/to glide in." *Une galoche* is a wooden clog; you're on your own for figuring that one out.

Wanna French kiss?
On se roule une pelle?
Literally, "to roll in a shovel." The word *baiser* is a real problem in French. Traditional dictionaries will tell you that it's a kiss—but that's only in older French. Today, *baiser* means to fuck or to screw, both in the sexual sense ("I fucked your mom") or in the mess-someone-up sense ("I fucked up your face").

What's up?
Quoi de neuf?

In English, when asked "what's up?" we usually give a one-word answer because, let's face it, nobody really cares in the U.S. But in France they'll assume you actually want to know how they're doing, and they'll expect you to give a real answer, too.

How's it goin'?
Ça va?

How you doin'?
Tu vas bien?

You doin' good today?
T'es en forme?

Long time, no see!
Ça fait longtemps, dis donc!

What're you up to?
Qu'est-ce que tu fabriques?

What's the word?
Quelles sont les nouvelles?

What the hell are you up to?
Qu'est-ce que tu fous?

What the hell are you doing here?
Qu'est-ce que tu fous là?

Watcha up to?
Qu'est-ce que tu me racontes?

> **Nothing much.**
> *Pas grand-chose.*
>
> **Same shit, different day.**
> *Comme d'hab'.*
>
> **Gettin' by.**
> *On se débrouille.*
>
> **Same old bullshit.**
> *Toujours le même bordel.*

How you been?
Alors, qu'est-ce que tu deviens?

So-so.
Comme ci, comme ça.

Same as always, man.
Ben, toujours pareil.

Good!
Ça roule!
Literally, "it rolls."

Great!
Ça gaze!

Just peachy!
J'ai la pêche!

Awesome!
Ça baigne!

Unstoppable!
Je pète le feu!
Literally, "I'm fartin' fire."

Bye!
Au revoir!

Bye.
Bye; Salut.

See ya.
Ciao.
Young people often use the Italian phrase.

I'm sailing out of here.
Je mets les voiles.

The floor is all yours.
Je dégage le plancher.

I'm gonna jet.
Je mets les gaz.

I'm cuttin' out.
Je m'éclipse.

See ya next time.
À la prochaine.

Catch ya on the flip side.
On se verra de l'autre côté.

Later.
À plus.

We'll bump into each other again sometime.
À un de ces quatre.

Catch ya tomorrow.
À demain.

GLOBALIZING FRENCH
LE FRANÇAIS À L'HEURE MONDIALE

French slang today is a grab bag of all the new influences changing life in France, from social media and apps to American movies and TV. Rap is also a source for underworld vocab, and terms from Arabic or African dialects have gone mainstream in big cities. Here are a few examples getting wide use, especially in Paris.

My hometown
Mon bled

Doc
Un toubib

A bit
Un chouïah

Coffee
Le caoua

What's up
Wesh
Wesh means "what" in Arabic, but works similar to "What up?" in English.

What's up, my brothers!
***Wesh** les frères!*

I swear
Wallah

I swear, you can't trust him!
***Wallah**, il est chelou, le mec!*
W'Allah means "before Allah," so it has the since of "I swear." It's interchangeable with *Je te jure*, as in *"Je t'jure, j'étais fracas!"* (I swear, I was fucked up!).

Call me.
On s'appelle.

Let's roll.
On bouge; On y va.

I'm out of here.
Je me casse; Je me tire.

Get a move on; Move your ass.
Bouge ton cul.

Get out of the way.
Bouge de là.

Get lost, you're gettin' on my nerves!
Dégage, tu me gonfles!

Why don't you call me sometime?
Appelle-moi; Téléphone-moi.

Send me an email/an IM/a text.
Balance-moi un mél/un SMS/un texto.

Text me.
Texte-moi.

Email me.
Envoie-moi un courriel.

Yo!
Oh!

The following expressions work really well to get people's attention.

Look!
Regarde!

Check that out!
Regarde-moi ça!

Dude!
Mec!

Hey, babe!
Salut, ma beauté!

C'mere for a sec.
Viens voir une minute.
In this case, the French generally use "minute" instead of "second."

I gotta tell you something.
J'ai un truc à te dire.

....

Sorry
Désolé(e)

French people aren't as quick to apologize as Americans, because the French **would rather die** (*plutôt crever!*) than acknowledge that they screwed up. For them, politeness is more about respecting formalities than making nice. But if they do apologize, they will say the following.

I'm sorry.
Je suis désolé(e).

I'm truly sorry.
Je suis vraiment désolé(e); Je suis navré(e).

Sorry I'm late.
Je suis désolé(e) d'être en retard.

Pardon me.
Pardon.

My bad.
Désolé; Autant pour moi.

My apologies.
Toutes mes excuses.

I fucked up!
J'ai merdé!

In the true French way, if you want to commiserate with someone without admitting any wrongdoing, try out one of these phrases:

That's the way it goes.
Ben, c'est comme ça.

That sucks!
Ça craint!

That's fucked up!
C'est dégueulasse!

But we only hooked up once!
Mais je ne l'ai niqué(e) qu'une fois!

Whoops! You're not my boyfriend.
Ola! T'es pas mon mec.

You poor thing.
Pauvre petit(e).

Shitty luck!
Pas de bol!; C'est la loose!
French mistakes "loose, looser" for the American "to lose, to be a loser."

Ouch!
Aïe!

Oh, shit!
Merde!

Excuse me
Excusez-moi

Where politeness really kicks in for the French is with work situations, between strangers, or when there's an age difference. With friends you can usually assume everything's fine. Still, between foreign languages and different cultures, misunderstandings happen pretty easily. So, to clean up after any major derpitude on your part, you might want to keep some of these phrases handy.

Excuse me.
Excusez-moi. (formal or plural)/*Excuse-moi.* (casual and singular)

No worries.
T'inquiète.

Don't worry 'bout him/her.
Ignore-le/la.

Drop it; Let's drop it.
Laisse béton.

'Scuse my shitty French.
Excuse mon français pourri.

Pardon my French!
Pardon, ça m'a échappé.

Can I get by here?
Ça te dérange pas si je passe?

Ever notice how nothing gets somebody angrier than asking them why they're so upset? So if you want to get somebody all worked up, just point out . . . how worked up they seem.

Chill! I didn't do it on purpose!
Putain, ça va, j'ai pas fait exprès!

Take it easy; Easy does it.
Vas-y mollo.
Also sometimes spelled *vas-y molo.*

Relax, no one ever died from that!
C'est bon, ça n'a jamais tué personne!

Don't make such a big deal out of it.
On va pas en faire tout un fromage.
Literally, "let's not turn this into cheese."

Don't shit your pants!
Te chie pas!

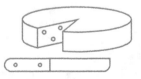

Can I at least get a word in?
Je peux en placer une?

Don't get your panties in a wad!
Détends ton string!
Literally, "don't wear your thong so tight!" (The French keep it sexy.)

....

Please
S'il te plaît/S'il vous plaît

If you need something, there are many ways of asking—some more polite than others.

Yo! Help me out!
S'iouplaît!

Can I get a little help?
Y a quelqu'un?

I'm on my knees.
Je suis à tes pieds.

I won't forget.
Je m'en rappellerai.

I owe you one.
Je te revaudrai ça.

I'm begging you.
Je t'en supplie.

Do me a favor.
Rends-moi service.

Could you do me a favor and tell your friend I think she's hot?
Tu pourrais pas me rendre service et dire à ta copine que je la trouve hyper bonne?

Would you please be so kind as to remove your knee from my balls.
Je te prierai de bien vouloir retirer ton genou de mes couilles.

Making friends
Soyons amis

Unlike in America, where it's common to talk to strangers in a bar or at school, in France people aren't used to this and will probably get a bit creeped out if you try it. Of course, this only applies to men—women are always welcome to walk up and introduce themselves. Generally, though, the best way to meet people is through groups rather than trying to go solo.

Nice to meet you.
Enchanté(e).

This is my first time in France.
C'est la première fois que je viens en France.

I'd like to meet some French people.
Je veux rencontrer des Français.

I don't understand French.
Je capte rien en français.

I don't understand a word you're saying.
Je pige que dalle.

This is my buddy.
C'est mon/ma pote.

Can you please tell your buddy that I think he's/she's cute?
Tu peux dire à ton/ta pote que je le kiffe?

Your girlfriend's hot.
Ta copine est vraiment bonne.

I love your boyfriend's hairy chest.
J'adore la poitrine poilue de ton mec.

Are you by yourself?
T'es tout(e) seul(e)?

What do you do in your free time?
Qu'est-ce que t'aimes faire?

INTRODUCING YOURSELF
SE PRÉSENTER

What's your name?
C'est quoi, ton nom?; Comment tu t'appelles?

My name's Jen.
Je m'appelle Jen.

I'm from the U.S.
Je suis américaine.

Yes, these are real breasts, and stop staring at them before I slam your face.
Oui, ce sont de vrais seins, et arrête de les mater avant que je t'en colle une.

I'm Brad.
Je suis Brad.

I'm from Colorado, and I'm hung like a horse.
Je viens du Colorado, et je suis monté comme un âne.
The French believe that donkeys *(ânes)* have bigger dicks than horses *(chevaux)*.
Why they've spent time thinking about this, we don't know.

Teach me some cuss words.
Apprends-moi des gros mots.

I like hanging with you.
J'aime passer du temps avec toi.

Can I bum a smoke?
Tu peux me filer une clope?

Is that guy you're with your dad?
C'est ton père, ce mec?

How old are you?
T'as quel âge?

Me, 30!? No way, it's just that we slept in the train station last night.
Moi, trente ans?! Mais non, c'est qu'on a créché à la gare hier soir!

Do you come here often?
Tu viens souvent ici?

Cells and selfies
Les portables et les selfies

The French aren't all that camera crazy, and have some negative stereotypes about people who take tons of pictures in public places, like at the Eiffel Tower or in parks and restaurants. But this attitude is starting to change, especially among the younger, tech-savvy crowd. Here are some useful terms and phrases.

A camera
Un appareil-photo

A digital camera
Un appareil-photo numérique; un numérique

A camcorder
Un camescope

A (computer) tablet
Une tablette

> I got a great panoramic with my **tablet**.
> *J'ai pris une super photo panoramique avec ma **tablette**.*

A cell phone
Un portable

> Did you take that picture with your **cell phone**?
> *T'as pris cette photo avec ton **portable**?*

Let's take a picture.
On prend une photo?

Can you take a picture of me?
Tu peux me prendre en photo?

Let's take **a selfie** with the Eiffel Tower in the background!
*On se fait **un selfie** devant la Tour Eiffel?*

A "selfie" is *un selfie*, a "selfie stick" is *un selfie stick*. In short, it remains obnoxious in both languages.

I'm a photographer for a top model agency and would like to photograph you.

Je suis photographe de mode et je travaille pour de grandes agences. Je peux te prendre en photo?

CHAPTER 2

Family & Folks
La Famille & les Potes

Friends
Les amis

Unlike in America, where we make "friends" by liking someone's pictures on Facebook but never talking to them in person, the French are old-fashioned or antisocial or something, and they want to, well, actually *know* you first. Whatever. If you do break through and hit it off with a French person, though, they'll stick with you.

A buddy; A pal
Un/une copain(e); Un/une pote
Copain and copine can be confusing. Mon copain means "my boyfriend," while un copain just means "a buddy."

>My **buddy** lives around here.
>*Mon **pote** habite près d'ici.*

A friend
Un/une ami(e)

>Here's to **good friends**!
>*Aux **bons amis**!*

Best friend
Meilleur ami/meilleure amie

>That asshole dumped your **best friend**?
>*Ce connard a largué ta **meilleure amie**?*

My besties
Mon/ma best

> Me and my **besties** are vacationing in Barcelona together!
> *Je prends mes vacances à Barcelone avec ma **best**!*

A school friend
Un/une camarade de classe

> Do you keep in touch with your old **school friends**?
> *Tu gardes le contact avec tes anciens **camarades de classe**?*

An acquaintance
Un/une connaissance

> There's **an acquaintance** I want you to meet.
> *J'ai **une connaissance** à te présenter.*

My boyfriend
Mon mec; mon copain

> My **boyfriend** has ginormous feet—you know what *that* means...!
> *Mon **mec** a des pattes monstrueuses—et tu sais ce que ça veut dire...!*

My man
Mon homme; mon mec

> My **man** can't clean the dishes to save his life.
> *Mon **homme** pourrait pas faire la vaisselle si sa vie en dépendait.*

My girlfriend
Mon amie; ma poule; ma nana; ma copine

> My **girlfriend** is the sweetest thing.
> *Ma **copine**, elle est la plus adorable de toutes.*

My dear
Mon chéri/ma chérie

> Cup o' tea, **my dear**?
> *Une tasse de thé, **mon chéri**?*

Roommate
Camarade de chambre

> My **roommate** is a disgusting asshole.
> *Mon **camarade de chambre** est un connard infect.*
>
> Dorms in France are mostly for foreign students. In big cities, though, high rents mean that more and more young people are sharing apartments. It's just like *Friends*—only poor, French, and not funny.

Housemate
Un/une colocataire; un/une coloc'

> Your **housemate** is cute.
> *Ton/Ta **coloc'** est mignon(ne).*

Coworker
Un/une collègue de travail

> Do you have any French **coworkers**?
> *Avez-vous des **collègues** français?*

American
Un ricain

The French think Americans are total badasses...and they think Americans are total idiots. In short, the French are pretty smart. The use of *ricain* can be perfectly friendly; *gros ricain* (big ol' Yank) means they're making fun of you.

....

Cool, funny shit
Des trucs fendards et cools

These expressions may be used in various contexts for things you like or think are funny, though the French don't laugh in public as much (or as loudly) as most Americans.

I know a **nice** little restaurant.
*Je connais un petit restau **sympa**.*

That bar has a **cool** DJ.
*Ce bar a un dj **super branché**.*

Your little brother can **hold his own**.
*Ton frangin **assure comme mec**.*
To make this feminine, you would say *Ta frangine assure comme nana.*

Daft Punk's last record is **great**.
*Le dernier disque de Daft Punk est **tarpin bien**.*
Tarpin is a recent all-occasions word for "very" or "a lot."

The production is **on point**.
*La prod' **est impec'**.*
Impec' is short for "impeccable."

Your roommate is **a crack-up**.
*Ton/Ta camarade de chambre est **rigolo(te)**.*

Your stupid jokes are **hysterical**.
*Tes blagues à la con sont **tordantes**.*

That commercial makes me **lose my shit**!
*Cette pub me fait **délirer grave**!*

You crazy asshole! Stop with the **jokes**! I'm gonna **piss my pants**.
*Enfoiré! Arrête tes **conneries**! Je vais **me pisser dessus**.*

Tell me some more **wise-cracks**, funny man.
*O, rigolo, balance-nous d'autres **vannes**.*

French gossip
Les ragots à la française

The French love to chill out at cafés and gossip about people; it's sort of a national sport.

He/She is...
Il/Elle est...

> **a stand-up guy**
> *un mec droit; un type correct*

> **a sweet girl**
> *une nana gentille*

a skank
une pouffiasse; une salope

a bitch
une connasse; une pétasse

a moron
un abruti

an airhead
une conne

a kiss-ass
un/une fayot(te)

a brown-noser
un lèche-cul
Literally, "a butt-licker."

a show-off
un frimeur/une frimeuse

a whiner
un/une geignard(e)

a manic-depressive
un/une cyclothymique

a good-for-nothing
un/une vaurien (ne); un/une looser

filthy rich
pété(e) de thunes; bourré(e) de fric

dirt poor
crève-la-dèche

Conversation starters
Briser la glace

While the French may have a centuries-old elite culture, highbrow references to Voltaire and Rimbaud won't get you very far if you're trying to make friends or get laid. Instead, add a few old-fashioned compliments to your banter and charm.

I love your accent.
J'adore ton accent.

What's that perfume you're wearing?
C'est quoi, ton parfum?

REGIONAL SLANG
L'ARGOT RÉGIONAL

People don't say "Git 'er done" in Sheboygan, Wisconsin, just like in Bryan, Texas, they don't call their butt "the pooper." And no one says *Laissez les bons temps rouler* outside of Louisiana! The same holds for France. Marseille, the wild city down on the Med', for example, has a strong Provençal and Occitan influence. Here's a few purely southern expressions that you will never hear "up north" on the Champs-Élysées:

We don't **fear nobody**.
*On **craint dégun**.*

His ex is real **clingy**.
*Son ex est une vraie **arapède**.*

Hey, **sleep-aholic**!
*Oh, **dormiasse**!*

Did you hear Bob got fired and his mutt got run-over? He's on a serious run of **hard luck**.
*T'as entendu qu'on a viré Bob et écrasé son clebs? Il a **la scoumougne**!*

Your shoes **stank** up my ride!
*Tes godasses m'ont **emboucané** la bagnole!*

That skate girl had a nasty **wipe-out**. She **fucked up** her elbow.
*Cette skateuse a salement **morflée**. Elle s'est **escagassé** le coude.*

He can **chat up** anyone!
*Il a la **tchatche**!*

My cousin is a total **wildman**!
*Mon cousin est un vrai **fada**!*

You look great in those jeans.
Comme tu assures dans ces jeans.

Do you prefer steak or seafood?
Tu préfères un steak ou des fruits de mer?

Can I buy you a drink?
Je peux t'offrir un verre?

Have we met before?
On s'est déjà rencontrés?

You have the most beautiful eyes.
T'as de beaux yeux.

Want to see my tattoo?
Tu veux voir mon tatouage?

Show me your new ink.
Montre-moi ton nouveau tatouage.

Wanna come back to my place?
Tu veux rentrer avec moi?

Formalities
Les formalités

Watch out for a few cultural differences. First, only medical doctors use "Dr." with their names; a Ph.D. in mass comm won't get you any special title in Lyon or Bordeaux. Second, when it comes to women, there's only *Mademoiselle* and *Madame*. While the use of *Mademoiselle* (any woman under 30) is starting to die out, there remains no equivalent to "Ms." in the French language.

Sir
Monsieur

Ma'am
Madame

Miss, Ms.
Mademoiselle

Dr.
Docteur

Mr. President
Monsieur le président

Judge
Monsieur/Madame le juge

If you get on better terms, you have some more informal options, too.

Doc
Toubib

Officer
Un flic; un keuf

Ol' man Dumas
Le père Dumas

Captain
Le commandant
This is used sarcastically, as in *Oui, mon commandant,* when your boyfriend tries to order you around.

....

Family
La famille

The concept of family remains pretty strong in France, especially in the South. People tend to be close to their entire family, including all the extended relatives, and kids often live with their parents well into adulthood until they get married or finally move in with their partners. But the French are slowly Americanizing: more and more, they come home after a few years, divorced and with a couple of kids in tow, to move back with their folks. Isn't it nice to see how much we have in common?

Dad
Papa

> My **dad** really needs to learn how to clear his browser history.
> *Mon **papa** a vraiment besoin d'apprendre comment effacer l'historique de son navigateur.*

Mom
Maman; ma rem

> My **mom** threw out my stash.
> *Ma **rem** a jeté ma réserve.*

My old man
Mon vieux; mon daron

> My **old man** loses his shit watching soccer.
> *Mon **vieux** pète les plombs en regardant le foot.*

My old lady
Ma vieille; ma vioque

In the U.S., "my old lady" refers to your wife; in France, it's your mom. In both countries, it's best when they're not the same person.

> My **old lady**'s got a tough life.
> *Ma **vioque** a la vie dure.*

My folks
Les croulants

This term puts your parents in the "I've fallen and I can't get up" category, since *croulant* means anything that is in the process of falling to ruins or collapsing.

Stepdad/Stepmom
Beau-père/Belle-mère

The same words are used for "father-in-law/mother-in-law"; context is the only way to know which is meant.

> My **stepdad** really cramps my style.
> *Mon **beau-père** me pourrit vraiment la vie.*

My bro'
Mon frangin

> My **brother** doesn't do shit.
> *Mon **frangin** est un glandeur.*

My sis'
Ma frangine

> Call **my sis'** a whore again and I'll kill you.
> *Si tu traites encore **ma frangine** de pute, je te tue.*

....

Funny characters
Drôles de personnages

The old-timer on the rickety bicycle with a beret and a baguette is long gone from the streets of Paris. But in big cities in particular, there's a whole cast of characters you can count on seeing sooner rather than later.

A wino
Le pochetron

A drunk
Un(e) ivrogne

A bum
Le/la clochard(e); le/la clodo; le/la SDF
SDF is *sans-domicile-fixe*, no fixed address.

A pervy old creep
Le vieux dégueulasse; un vieux pervers

> That **pervy old creep** groped me in the subway.
> *Ce **vieux dégueulasse** m'a empoigné le nibard dans le métro.*
> Literally, "took a fistful of tit."

Shady person
Louche; chelou

> My next-door neighbor looks like a **shady character**.
> *Mon voisin a l'air **chelou**.*

A thug
Un voyou; une racaille; une caillera
Like "thug" in English, *racaille* and *caillera* can be racist code; in the French context, it is brandished about in references to Black and North African

immigrants living in the suburban housing projects. With a history dating back to the 1800s, *voyou* remains more ethnically neutral.

A spoiled rich kid
Un fils/une fille à papa

> **Spoiled rich kids** are annoying as shit.
> *Les **fils à papa** sont chiants comme tout.*

A redneck
Un pequenot; un blaireau
The latter is French for the animal "badger."

> Goddamn racist **redneck**!
> *Putain de **pequenot** raciste!*

A country hick
Un plouc

> That **country hick** hides a wicked pool game.
> *Ce **plouc** cache un méchant jeu de billards.*

A ladies' man
Un tombeur; un homme à femmes

A good ol' boy (in a positive sense)
Un bon bougre

> He's a regular **good ol' boy**.
> *C'est un vrai **bon bougre**.*

A jock
Le sportif/la sportive

> That **jock** has cauliflower ears from playing rugby.
> *Ce **sportif** a les oreilles en chou-fleur à cause du rugby.*

A horndog
Le queutard

> That **horndog** jumps anything that moves.
> *Ce **queutard** saute sur tout ce qui bouge.*

A slut
Une grosse pute/une poufiasse

Everyday folks
Le commun des mortels

Each country has its own stereotypes that the media and public use all the time. Here are a few clues about French stereotypes, so that you'll recognize who you're dealing with.

White trash
Les beaufs

Being white trash isn't so much a question of money as it is of style—though usually they don't have much of either. For the guys, they have only one obsession that doesn't involve alcohol or ass: their car. The *beauf* has a strong preference for French automakers and cars (especially the old, boxy Renault 12 of the '70s, or a used Peugeot 405 from the '90s). He spends most of his salary (if he works at all) on accessories to make his car "unique," many of which are borrowed from the U.S.: hanging dice, fake fur covering the steering wheel, top-of-the-line car stereo with speakers taking up the entire trunk. When he hits his midlife crisis, he'll prefer a ponytail to the American mullet, but he'll unbutton his shirt to show tufts of hair and fake gold chains, and will sport bun-hugger pants. He's convinced he's a player, so he goes heavy on the French version of Old Spice (Drakkar Noir). He can't be bothered to talk to his girlfriend, but he'll start a fight if anybody else tries to. He has a favorite bar, and is incredibly loyal in friendship...when he's not drunk and trying to bust a bottle over your head.

The Bible-thumpers
Les culs bénis

Literally, these are the "ass-blessed," also known as *les bigots* (fire and brimstone dads) and *les bigotes* (church ladies). These French believers, usually Catholic, are fanatical in their faith. They're starting to make a comeback, though percentage-wise there are more atheists in France than in the U.S., and the fastest-growing religion is Islam. The *culs bénis* go to mass every week, prepare for Communion, volunteer at their parish, attend private Catholic schools, and join the Boy Scouts or Girl Scouts.

The commuters
Les métro-boulot-dodo

Making fun of these people is kind of harsh, because it's a hard life. You wake up at 5 a.m. in your small, suburban apartment while it's still dark outside. You get dressed, grab a coffee, walk 15 minutes to the regional train, stand in the onboard crowd for 30 minutes, transfer to the subway (*métro*), take it for another 45, and soon you're at your desk for another day at the job (*boulot*). Nine hours later, reverse paths, microwave a frozen dinner, watch the news, and hit the sack to snooze (*dodo*, from *dormir*, to sleep). At the same time, though, when you see them asleep on the train with their heads all the way back and their mouths wide open, it's tempting to imagine what would happen if you dropped a goldfish down the hatch.

Hippies
Les baba cools

The '60s were a big deal in France, probably even more so than in the U.S. The student movement of May 1968 almost brought down the government. Many of the kids who participated in and drove the movement are still around today, easily recognizable by their hippie accessories (incense, beads, tie-dye dresses, blonde dreads). But you probably won't see too many because they're more likely found living in teepees and yurts out in the countryside.

The cow pies
Les bouseux

These are the farmers who come into town and stand next to you in line at the bank. Even if you don't see them coming, you can smell them: *Une bouse* is a cow pie, so they're called *bouseux* because of the cow shit splashed all the way up their rubber boots.

They're the last symbols of old France, with accents that make a barefoot Kentucky minister sound like an Oxford grad, and driving habits that make a tractor on the highway seem fast.

The bo-hos
Les bobos

Most of these bohemian "68ers" (*soixante-huitards*) did eventually get tired of eating grain cereals, tripping to sitar music, and doing laundry by hand in a creek. And, surprisingly, many of them ended up getting quite wealthy. They've been divorced several times, and the moms want to be best friends with their daughters, and the dads want to sleep with girls their daughters' age. At the same time, though, they see themselves as enlightened and cultured, with esoteric spiritual beliefs and an absolute devotion to recycling. The politically conscious *bobos* usually have an eccentric signature gimmick, like Rollerblading to work, and belong to what's known as the *Gauche caviar*—left-wingers who speak with great passion about the suffering of the poor...while eating caviar in their spectacular Parisian duplex apartments. This subculture is despised as intensely as that of hipsters in the U.S.

The rich folk
Les costume-cravate

Literally the "suit and ties," but in France it's not synonymous with "the Feds." Often graduates of French or American business schools, they are executives (*les cadres*) employed by corporations. It's never been terribly cool to talk about how much money you make or to splash it around in people's faces, but *les costume-cravate* are trying to change that. Often pretentious, individualist, and driven by money only, they are so wrapped up in their success that they won't realize you're laughing at them.

The upper crust
Les bourges

Some of the *costume-cravate* join the ranks of the *bobos* when they turn 50; terrified of getting old, they suddenly discover a passion for windsurfing, travel to Third World countries, and switch to solar power. The others consolidate their money into social prestige by veering conservative: they become *bourges* (short for *bourgeois*). They'll do everything possible to smell like old money, and will disdain anyone who got rich the way they did. The fathers will be disciplinarians, the mothers uptight and formal. It's not easy to grow old gracefully when you're rich—but it probably still beats being poor.

Chapter 3

Booze, Bars, & Clubs
Bibine, Bars, & Boîtes de nuit

The French have more ways to say "party" than the ancient Greeks had gods. For starters, there's *la fête, la bringue, la java, la noce, la bomba, la nouba, la bamboche, la bamboula, la fiesta, la teuf, la ribote, la goguette, la ribouldingue*.... So prep by mastering these party words and then go get ready to go out!

What's the plan?
C'est quoi, le plan?

Do you have **plans** tonight?
*T'as des **projets** ce soir?*

You goin' out?
Tu sors?

What're you doin'?
Tu fais quoi?

Let's **go out** tonight!
*Ce soir, **on sort**!*

Let's **hit** the bars.
*On **se prend** les bars.*

Are you busy tonight?
Tu fais quelque chose ce soir?

I'm bored shitless.
Je me fais chier.

Let's **have a drink** somewhere.
Allons boire un coup quelque part.

....

Party!
C'est la fête!

The minimum drinking age in France is 18, but no one actually pays attention to it. As long as you can see over the counter, you can buy booze. Same thing with clubs. As long as you're dressed right and looking good, the bouncer will let you in, regardless of age. And most places stay open all night, so there's no need to pound your weight in Jägerbombs the second you make it to the bar.

Party animal
Un fêtard; un bringueur; un noceur

I feel like **partying**!
Je suis d'humeur à faire la fête!

I'm up for anything.
Je suis prêt(e) à tout.

I wanna **have a great time** tonight.
Je veux m'éclater ce soir.

We're gonna bring it!
On va tout déchirer!

I'm gonna **let loose**!
Je vais me déchaîner!
Literally, "get unchained."

I'm fed up with beer. Let's go dancing for once.
J'en ai marre de la bière. Allons danser pour une fois.

Let's go to a **club**.
Allons en boîte.

This place is **poppin'**.
Ça chauffe ici.

That's a **badass beat**!
C'est un putain de groove, ça!

Let's get it crackin'!
On attaque!

Let's get down!
Mettons le feu!
Literally, "let's get it lit."

Should we go **bar-hopping**?
On se fait une virée?

Let's pull an **all-nighter**.
Faisons nuit blanche.
Literally, a "white night," meaning to stay out 'til the sun comes up.

THE BOUNCER
LE VIDEUR

Technically, a bouncer never actually rejects anyone. Instead, he asks if you've got the "club membership" or tells you that it's a private party. After that, though, if you bug him he'll probably make it easier for you to understand.

Look, you dress like an American. Now **get the fuck out of here** before I explode your face.
Écoute, t'es sapé comme un gros ricain. Alors casse-toi avant que je t'explose la tête.

Chill, dude. When you **get worked up**, you look like a real **dickhead**.
Calme-toi, vieux. Quand tu te fous en rogne, ça fait franchement tête de vier.

***

Go fuck yourself. I'm about to kill you.
Va te faire enculer. Je vais te massacrer.

Whatever. Shove **your membership card** up your ass, good and deep.
Comme tu veux, mais la carte de membre, tu peux te la carrer dans le cul, bien profond.

Want **another drink?**
Tu veux un autre verre?

Let's...
Allons...

> **hit on some guys**
> *branchons des mecs*

> **hit on some girls**
> *branchons des gonzesses/des filles/des nanas*

> **get laid** (with a guy)
> *nous taper des mecs*

> **get laid** (with a girl)
> *nous taper des gonzesses/des filles/des nanas*

If you're at a French club and some fugly schmo starts hitting on you, don't make eye contact and *definitely* don't flash a smile. What is only a polite hello in the U.S. translates to "come and get it" in Paris or Strasbourg.

Don't be such a buzz kill.
Ne nous casse pas les couilles!
Literally, "don't bust our balls."

Why do French guys always **check themselves out** in the mirror when they dance?
Pourquoi les mecs français se regardent tous danser dans les miroirs?

Where French people get down
Où les Français sortent

Bars, cafés, and pharmacies are the most common businesses found in a typical French city. Seriously, it's bizarre how many pharmacies there are in France. It's like everyone has cheap health care that pays for their drugs or something. Err—, wait; they do.

Let's go to...
Allons à/au/dans...

a bar
un bar

a bar and cigarette shop
un bar-tabac

a pub or tavern
un pub; un pub irlandais

dive bar
troquet

a wine bar
un bar à vins

a café
un café

Café refers to either the drink (coffee) or the place, or both. A cool thing about cafés in France is that they always have beer on tap, as well as a small bar, and it's usually cheaper to drink there.

a café-theater
un café-théâtre

You can eat and drink there, but you can also buy a ticket for a comedy play or stand-up act.

a music bar
un café-concert

Usually jazz, traditional French music, or world music, with high cover or drink prices.

THE THREE "NEVERS" OF FRENCH DISCOS
LES TROIS "JAMAIS" EN DISCOTHÈQUE

1. Never show up at the door in a group of all guys.

2. Never show up wearing shorts or flip-flops (unless you're a woman).

3. Never assume you will be able to take a shit at a disco (it won't be possible, trust us).

---

a disco
la discothèque

French discos don't open until 11 p.m. at the earliest, but nobody really shows up until about 1. There's usually a pricey cover charge that includes a free drink, but women can negotiate to get in free. Getting in has nothing to do with age and everything to do with looks (and, unfortunately, sometimes race—some French discos have been closed for racial profiling). All French discos use bouncers to select the clientele and take care of security.

a nightclub
une boîte de nuit; un night-club

More discreet and quiet than a disco, often private

a cabaret
un cabaret

Venues like the Pigalle district's famous Crazy Horse have Vegas-style shows with, depending on the place, a meal and/or champagne...as well as varying degrees of nudity.

a whore bar
un bar à putes

a food hut; a food truck; a late-night fast-food kebab place
une baraque à frites; un kiosque à sandwichs; un kebab

France had after-hours food trucks long before they sprouted like mushrooms in Austin and Portland. Americans will be disappointed by French pizza; for post-beer binge comfort food, go with a *kebab-frites* (a kebab sandwich in a thick pita pocket with lots of greasy steak fries) or a *merguez-frites* (another open sandwich of spicy lamb sausage with matchstick fries directly on top and a couple shakes of super-hot Harissa sauce from Tunisia).

an "American-style" bar
un bar américain

This is a special kind of bar with hostesses (*hôtesses*), who are basically in-house escort girls. Their job is to run up your tab as much as possible by ordering expensive bottles of Champagne. They love to rip off tourists and they have huge bouncers to make sure you forget about trying to get your money back. In other words, it's a really shitty place to hang out.

a swingers club
un club libertin; une boîte échangiste

These semi-underground clubs (often, in fact, literally underground, in medieval-looking basements) feature about 50 naked people getting down in a series of rooms, some of which will inevitably include spastic imitations of BDSM practices. They are illegal in the U.S. and, well, kind of illegal in France. What used to be one of Paris's worst-kept secrets is now a hangout spot for jaded male celebrities looking for a thrill. So on any given night you might see a bunch of former child stars bumpin' uglies with a gaggle of Parisian "models," while some creepy guy in leather pants waves around a riding crop.

This party is **lit**!
*Cette bringue est **enflammée**!*

This neighborhood looks **sketchy**.
*Ce quartier **craint**, non?*

Should we go somewhere else?
On bouge?

> I'm down. This place **sucks**.
> *Ça me va. C'est **nul** ici.*

Should we **get out** of here?
*On **se tire**?*

Should we **bounce**?
*On **se casse**?*

Let's stay for **one more drink**.
*Prenons **un dernier verre**.*

Boozing it up
Beuveries

France's love affair with wine means you can buy it pretty much anywhere, including great bottles at reasonable prices in supermarkets, which would be kinda like buying Dom Pérignon at your local 7-Eleven. Stay away, however, from those plastic bottles of wine. They're criminally cheap for a reason, and they make you regurgitate showers of pink chunder. Beer is more popular in the north and northeast of the country.

Cheers!
Santé!; Tchin-tchin!

To good friends!
Aux amis!

Should we grab a quick beer?
On s'en jette une?

You got **beer on tap**?
*Vous avez des **bières à la pression**?*

Gimme a...
Donne-moi...

> **beer**
> *de la bière*

> **cheap beer**
> *de la bibine*

> **glass of beer, please**
> *un demi, s'il vous plaît*

> **pint**
> *un sérieux; une pinte*

> **liter of beer**
> *un formidable; un litre*
> The French equivalent of the American 40, served in a big-ass glass mug.

> **bottle opener**
> *un tire-bouchon*

Let's pound these shots.
On va se les faire cul sec.

Hey bartender, **a round** for my friends.
*M'sieu! **une tournée** pour mes amis.*

Chug! Chug! Chug!
Eh glou! Eh glou! Eh glou!

We're popping a **bottle of bubbly!**
*On fait péter une **roteuse**!*
Literally, "a burper."

....

Booze
Bibine

Many French people, especially in the countryside, still make their own brandy and cognac. Quite often it amounts to "craft-brewing" jet fuel. Study-abroad folks should be forewarned. If you have a host family, at some point they're liable to bring it out at the end of a meal that already featured four different wines. It's easy to spot: it'll be in a clear bottle with no label or just a taped-on piece of paper with a date scribbled on it and a pear or apricot floating at the bottom. Next to these concoctions, Mezcal tastes like candy. And it's *really* bad manners to wimp out on a glass, as it's the house tradition to enjoy with guests.

Pour me...
Versez-moi...

> *un pastis; un pastaga (in the south)*
> You add a little water and an ice cube to this anis liqueur and the yellowish liqueur turns white. The sweet flavor makes it treacherous. Drink a bunch of these, and you'll have a blinding headache like you've never known.

> *un panaché*
> A lemonade beer tastes great, especially when it's hot or in the afternoon.

> *un despérado, un despy'*
> A beer with a dash of syrupy tequila flavor in it.

> *une eau-de-vie*
> a brandy

> *une Poire William*
> It takes 61 pounds of pears to make 2 liters of this pear brandy!

un Calvados; un Calva

Apple brandy. If you've been paying attention, you'll know what region makes this.

un trou normand

This Calvados-type drink, which translates to "The Norman Hole," is lethal. After a really heavy meal, you're supposed to throw this burning mixture down the hatch in order to sear a hole through your just-digested food to make room for dessert. Try this once and you'll understand why so many old-timers in the French countryside have cirrhosis.

If you don't have a pressing need to shred your liver with a Norman Hole, you can always get mixed drinks and cocktails at nightclubs—though they're not as popular in France, and most bars don't serve them. Mojitos and Cuba Libres are familiar to many in the U.S., but here are a few exotic favorites you probably don't know:

Une tequila frappée

For a tequila banger, mix tequila and tonic water, place a coaster over it, bang it on the table, and guzzle it down as it fizzes. Chase with lime and salt.

Un Kiss Cool

Curaçao and Sambuca in a shot glass. Swirl it around in your mouth as long as you can stand it (it'll burn), swallow it down, and then inhale the vapors.

La Soupe de champagne

"Champagne soup" is champagne, lime juice, and Cointreau.

Le Vagin

"The Vagina" is a bit of lime juice in the bottom of a shot glass, a couple fingers of apricot brandy, and a maraschino cherry. Shoot it and bite into the cherry.

Wine
Vin

Where does Champagne come from? Well, who's buried in Grant's Tomb? French wines bear the name of the region where they're produced. Bordeaux in the southwest and Burgundy (Bourgogne) in the middle of the country are the most famous reds. But you can find some cheaper but still-solid reds from the Marseille region, Côtes du Rhône.

May I have a glass of...?
Puis-je avoir un verre de... ?

> **red wine**
> *vin rouge*
>
> **white wine**
> *vin blanc*
>
> **rosé wine**
> *vin rosé*
>
> **rotgut wine**
> *pinard*
>
> **Champagne, or sparking wine**
> *Champagne*
>
> **A small glass** of red wine
> *Un ballon de rouge*

Wine coolers don't exist in France but there is something called a "*kir*," which is wine mixed with another alcohol. The standard kir is two-thirds white wine (Bourgogne Aligoté) and one-third *crème de cassis* (black currant liqueur). There are a bunch of spin-offs and they're all delicious, especially as a premeal drink (*un apéritif*).

> *Kir normand*
> Cider with *crème de cassis*
> The Normandy region grows apples.
>
> *Kir cardinal*
> Red Bordeaux with *crème de cassis*
> Named for the bright red uniform worn by cardinals in the Catholic church.
>
> *Kir royal*
> Champagne with *crème de cassis*
>
> *Kir impérial*
> Champagne with *crème de framboise* (raspberry)

Le Double K
The Krushchev Kir (white wine, vodka, *crème de cassis*)

Totally wasted
Défoncé(e)

When you get to use the expressions in this section, it'll probably already be too late to look them up.

I'm starting to get...
Je commence à être...

>**a little tipsy**
>*un peu gris(e)*

>**a bit drunk**
>*un peu saoul(e)*

>**buzzed**
>*bourré(e)*

>**sick**
>*malade*

That dumb tourist is...
Ce con de touriste est...

>**smashed**
>*fracassé(e)*

>**drunk off his ass**
>*complètement dans les vapes*

>**completely fucked up; stoned; (also) insane in the brain**
>*complètement à l'ouest*
>Literally, "way out West."

>**about to puke**
>*sur le point de gerber*

I'm gonna get ripped!
*Je vais me **fracasser**!*

We got hella **wasted**!
*On a pris une de ces **cuites**!*

She's really **lit**!
*Elle est complètement **allumée**!*

We're so **fucked up**!
*On est complètement **défoncés**!*

Wow, did you see her **projectile vomit**?!
*Waow, mais t'as vu ce **bouquet de gerbe**?!*
Literally, "bouquet of vomit."

Last night I was so **wasted,** I had to pee in the sink.
*Hier soir j'étais tellement **défoncée**, j'ai dû pisser dans l'évier.*

Oh, great, **baby your hangover** on the only day I don't **work**.
*Ouais, c'est ça, **cuve ta cuite**, le seul jour où je **bosse** pas.*

Taking it easy
Relaxation

After a few nights of nonstop partying in Caen or Angers, you'll be glad to know the following:

Tonight I....
Ce soir je....

>> **am toast**
>> *suis crevé(e)*

>> **am going home early**
>> *vais rentrer tôt*
>> (Ha! How'd that plan work out for you?!)

>> **can't, I got work to do**
>> *peux pas, j'ai du **taff***

>> **wanna watch TV**
>> *veux mater la télé*

wanna catch a movie
veux me faire un cinoche

am gonna kick back
vais me la filer tranquille

am gonna chill out
vais me la couler douce

am just hangin' out at home
traîne à la maison

am not gonna do squat
vais rien foutre

am gonna just **jack around**
*vais **branler que dalle***

am gonna **dick off**
*vais **glander***

Weed
L'herbe

Paris is not Amsterdam when it comes to drugs. The French government cracks down pretty hard, and people are cautious about it on the streets. Nonetheless, a lot of French smoke weed and hash. A few grow it at home, but most comes from Morocco. No guarantees on the quality. And, as everywhere else in the world, it pays to know your dealer. Bogus ones will try to screw you over and sell you mixtures of oregano and wax that will have you on the toilet all night.

Weed
L'herbe; La fumette
The former is also used inverted, *le beuh*. The latter is literally, "the small smoke," because French weed is weaker than hash.

A joint
Un joint
A joint can also be *un oinj*; a spliff is *un spliff*; a blunt is *un blunt*. (You're welcome.)

A J
Un pétard; un beuze

Hash
Le hasch; le haschisch; du shit

Pass the **hash joint**.
*Passe-moi le **bédo**.*
This often implies it is cheap stuff.

To grow Maryjane
Faire pousser de la Marie-Jeanne

My aunt's an **old hippie**; she grows weed on her balcony.
*Ma tante est une **vieille baba cool**; elle fait pousser de l'herbe sur son balcon.*

Do you know a **dealer**?
*Tu peux nous trouver un **dealer**?*

Are you holding?
T'as que'que chose pour nous?

Do you know where I can get some stuff?
Tu sais où je peux en avoir?

I'm getting a little **stoned**.
*Je commence à être un peu **défoncé(e)**.*

I'm spaced.
Je plane.

Shit, I'm really fucking **baked**. I'm gonna take **a nap**.
*Putain, je suis complètement **dans la ouate**. Je vais faire **un somme**.*

I've got the munchies something fierce.
Il faut absolument que je grignote quelque chose.

I was so high, I ate a pound of cookie dough.
J'étais tellement à l'ouest, j'ai bouffé 500 grammes de pâte à galettes.

Hard stuff
La drogue dure

While smoking weed is somewhat tolerated in France, coke or Ecstasy will get you jail time. Definitely a case of "buyer beware." So if anybody asks, you didn't learn these words from us.

Coke
La coca

Crack
Le crack

White powder
La poudre blanche

A line
Une ligne

A rail
Un rail

Pills
Des pilules

> We took some **pills** at the Rennes rave fest.
> *On a gobé des **pilules** au festival rave de Rennes.*

Man, you're an **addict**.
*Mon vieux, t'es **accro'**.*

X, molly
L'ecsta, le molly

Chapter 4

Sexy Body, Ugly Body
La Belle & la Bête

The French sexy
Le français sexy

He/She is...
Il/Elle est...

> **handsome** (guys)
> *beau*
>
> **a good-lookin' kid**
> *beau gosse/beau mâle* (male)
> *belle plante/belle nana* (female)
>
> **beautiful** (girls)
> *belle*
>
> **cute**
> *mignon(ne)*
>
> **really cute** (girls)
> *craquante*
>
> **"model" hot** (guys)
> *une gravure de mode*
>
> **pretty** (girls)
> *jolie*

totally hot (girls)
bandante
Literally, "makes you hard" (just to see her). Using a direct translation of "hot" (*chaude*) for a girl can also mean "horny."

sexy
sexy

stylish
à la mode

really fashionable
glamour

hip
branché(e)
Literally, "plugged in," "connected."

trendy
tendance

He/She has...
Il/Elle a...

a lean **face**
*un **visage** fin*

a friendly or likable **face**
*une bonne **bouille***

a good "**mug**"
*une bonne **gueule***

a hot **figure**
*une très belle **silhouette***

good **measurements**
*de bonnes **mensurations***

The French nasty
La laideur française

If you're a sucker for those TV commercials that always show the French as ultra-stylish and slim, you're in for a big surprise. The ugly are a well-represented species in France.

He/She has...
Il/Elle a...

> **an egghead**
> *une tête d'œuf*
>
> beady **eyes**
> *de petits yeux*
>
> a nasty "**grill**"
> *une tronche pas possible*
>
> a **stubby body** and short legs
> *un corps trapu et de petites jambes*
>
> **a tangled mop of hair**
> *une sale tignasse*
>
> **a bad figure**
> *mal foutu(e)*
>
> a tiny **head**
> *une petite tête*
>
> **a big head**
> *une grosse tête*
>
> To *have* a "big head" can mean that you're conceited, just as in English. But if you say that someone *is* a "big head," it means that they're either really smart or a total nerd.
>
> **a face made for smacking**
> *une tête à claques*
>
> A great expression for people whose poseur smiles are so smug and vapid that it spoils their looks.

Your girlfriend looks like an **Orangina bottle**.
*Ta copine ressemble à une **bouteille d'Orangina**.*
The French way to say, "She is flat-chested but has some junk in the trunk."

Your boyfriend has a **beer belly**.
*Ton mec a un **bébé Kro**.*
"Kro" is short for Kronenbourg, the most common brand of French beer. In English, this would be like saying, "He's expecting a baby Bud."

You gotta do something about those **love handles**.
*Il faut que tu perdes ces **poignets d'amour**.*
The French magazine *Paris-Match* once tried to curry favor with President Sarkozy by publishing a shirtless photo of him with his love handles photoshopped out.

Her head is bigger than her body.
Sa tête est plus grosse que son corps.

Did you **comb your hair** with a fire cracker?
*Tu **t'es coiffé** avec un pétard?*

He/She is...
Il/Elle est...

> **ugly**
> *laid(e)*
>
> **homely**
> *un/une laideron(ne); un/une mocheté(e)*
>
> **so ugly he/she attracts animals**
> *tellement laid(e) qu'il/elle attire les bêtes*
>
> **a fat slob** (for guys)
> *un gros porc*
>
> **dirty**
> *sale*
>
> **filthy**
> *crade*

a dog
un thon
Literally, "a tuna."

a fat, stuffed sausage
un boudin

a nasty cow
une grognasse

beastly (guys)
ignoble

completely gross (guys)
immonde
Literally, "not of this world."

nasty (guys)
vilain

Body types
Types de corps

He/She is...
Il/Elle est...

tall
grand(e)

well-built (girls)
bien foutue

buff (guys)
bien baraqué; bien tanqué; costaud

little/short
petit(e)

short
court(e) sur pattes
Literally, "short on their paws."

a midget
un/une nain(e)

frail (guys), **delicate** (girls)
délicat(e)

a bag of bones
un sac d'os

hunchback
bossu(e)

tanned
bronzé(e)

pale
pale, palot

long-haired
chevelu(e)
More for hippies than cavemen types.

hairy
poilu(e)

chunky, chubby
grassouillet(te)

fat
gros/grosse

skinny
maigre; maigrichon(ne)

The can
Les chiottes

There's nothing worse than being abroad and not knowing how to find a public toilet when you realize that the pâté was a day too old. In France, that may mean finding *Madame Pipi* (literally, "the Pee Lady") and having to shell out a few coins, especially for a sit-down.

Where is/are...?
Où...?

the restrooms
sont les toilettes; les WC; les sanitaires

the john
est le petit coin

the toilet paper
est le papier cul
Literally, "butt paper."

the TP
est le PQ

the bathroom attendant
est Madame Pipi
In tourist cities especially, it's common to have bathroom attendants charge for access to public restrooms in large public facilities (number two will cost you more). And if you find one without a *Madame Pipi*, don't count on there being any *PQ*.

the "Turkish" toilets
les chiottes à la turque
Squat-and-shit toilets, common in older restaurants and bars, consist of a hole in the porcelain floor with two raised footpads to stand on. Unless you're wearing rain gear, make sure you stand and back up a bit when you pull the overhead chain to flush. And it gets worse: In many of these older toilets, the lights are on a timer. If you don't finish fast enough, you'll find yourself stranded in the pitch dark, on a slippery surface, with your pants around your ankles.

the public toilet
les toilettes; le WC public
On main streets in big cities like Paris and Toulouse, you'll find space-age bathrooms (tall, shiny cylinders) right in the middle of the sidewalk. You put your coins in the slot, the door slides open, and you walk in. Do not—we repeat, do not—slide in after someone else to try to use it after them for free. After the door closes, it locks and there's an automatic cleaning process where you'll get doused and fumigated.

Shitting
Chier

When "nature calls" in France, it's just that: natural. Few French people are embarrassed about pissing and shitting, the way they are in the U.S. When your French host starts to describe his or her digestion to you in great detail, you'll know you're part of the family.

Frank **stinks up** the can every single time.
*Franck **empeste** les chiottes à chaque fois.*

Don't go in there, some jerk blew his **ass** out.
*Surtout n'entrez pas, y a un connard qui s'est défoncé le **fion**.*

It's not that classy to leave **skidmarks** in the bowl.
*Ce n'est pas très classe de laisser des **traces de freinage** au fond de la cuvette.*

STINKIN' IT UP
EMPESTER

When traveling in a foreign country, sometimes your friends forget to shower, and just about every part of their body can get pretty ripe. The expression "*il pue de la...*" allows you to add in whatever body part you need, to tell them just how stank they really are.

*Chris pue des **pieds**.*
Chris's **feet** stink.

*Jean-Pierre pue du **cul**.*
Jean-Pierre's **ass** smells nasty.

*Pam pue de la **moule**.*
Pam's **pussy** is rank.
The U.S.'s "bearded clam" is a "mussel" (with its little tuft) in France.

*Gérard **pue de la gueule; du bec**.*
Gérard's got **stink-breath**.
Literally, stinks "from the muzzle," "the (bird) beak."

You just stepped in **shit**!
*Tu viens de marcher dans la **merde**!*

I gotta....
Je dois....

> **go poo**
> *faire caca*

> **take a dump**
> *caguer; chier*

> **drop a bomb**
> *couler une bielle* (a rod); *couler un bronze*

> **wipe my ass**
> *me torcher le cul*

I've got a bitch of a need **to shit**.
*J'ai une putain d'envie de **chier**.*

I'm about to crap my pants.
Je vais me faire au froc.

I'm prairie-dogging it.
J'ai le cigare au bout des lèvres.
Literally, "the cigar is at the edge of my lips."

I just shit a snake.
J'ai chié un serpent.
This describes a long, skinny turd.

That shit ripped my **bunghole** apart.
*Je me suis défoncé le **trou de balle**.*
Literally, "bullet hole or wound."

Man, I was so scared on that flight that **I was shitting bricks**.
*Mec, j'ai eu tellement la trouille dans l'avion que **j'ai chié des lames de rasoir** en travers.*
Literally, "shitting out razor blades sideways."

That cassoulet gave me the runs/the shits.
Ce cassoulet m'a donné la chiasse.

BODY BLOWS
TRAVAILLER LE CORPS

English insults often draw on sexual aggression while French mockery relies on references to bodily functions.

That's a shitty thing to say.
T'es chiant(e) de dire ça.

Betty thinks her shit doesn't stink.
Betty pète plus haut que son cul.
Literally, "Betty farts from higher than her asshole."

He thinks he's the shit.
Il se prend pas pour une merde.

You're a sack of shit.
Espèce de sac à merde.

Go fuck yourself.
Je te chie sur la gueule.
Literally, "I shit in your face."

Eat shit.
Mange merde.

I wasn't born yesterday.
Je n'ai pas de la merde aux yeux.
Literally, "I don't have shit covering my eyes."

He's such a little shit.
C'est un petit merdeux.

His sister's a whiny brat.
Sa sœur est une pisseuse.
Literally, "a bed wetter."

This town is the armpit of the universe.
*Ce bled est le **trou du cul** du monde.*
Literally, "the **butthole** of the world."

You'll end up with **the travel shits** if you drink Paris **tap water**.
*Tu auras **la turista** si tu bois **l'eau du robinet** à Paris.*

Nothing better than a really good shit.
Rien de tel qu'une bonne grosse merde.

In fact, shitting is so great that at least one French proverb claims it's better than love.

> **Love may burn like fire, but the need to shit is the greatest desire.**
> *L'amour est un feu qui dévore mais l'envie de chier est plus forte encore.*

Burping and farting
Roter et péter

English insults use a lot of sexual images ("Screw you," "I'll fuck you up"), while French insults tend toward the scatological. So all those ridiculous insults in *Monty Python and the Holy Grail*, like "I fart in your general direction," are actually barely tweaked, *real* French expressions.

A burp
un rot

To burp
roter

Did your girlfriend just **belch**?
*C'est ta copine qu'a **roté**?*

A fart
Un pet

To have gas
Avoir des gaz

Who farted?
Qui c'est qui a pété?
One of the most important sentences in any language.

Pierre ripped one.
Pierre a lâché une caisse.

SPECIALTY FARTS
PETS SPÉCIAUX

The SBD (silent but deadly)
La louffe

The skidmark fart
Le pet foireux; le pet coulant

The liquid fart
Le pet liquoreux

The mudslide fart
Le pet merdeux

The "firework" fart
La pétarade
These are loud, but odorless and dry.

The creaky door fart
La Louise
These farts are long, thin, and whistle-y, like "LooooooouulllllZzeeuh!"
The biggest selling indie rock band of all time in France was called "Louise Attaque."

Someone **dropped an atomic bomb.**
*Y'en a un qui a **lâché une bombe atomique**.*

That's not **my smell.**
*C'est pas **mon odeur**.*

To slip or slide out like **a fart on wax paper**
*Glisser comme **un pet sur une toile cirée***
You know how—despite our best intentions, of course—farts sometimes just seep right out? Well, the French use this phenomenon to describe things that slip and slide.

To slip or slide out like a nun's fart against a stained glass window
Glisser comme un pet de bonne sœur sur le vitrail d'une cathédrale

Pissing
Pisser

In France, instead of "pissing in the wind" you "piss in a violin" *(pisser dans un violon)*.

I gotta....
Je dois....

> **take a piss**
> *pisser*
>
> **tinkle**
> *faire pipi*
>
> **take a leak**
> *vidanger*
> Literally, "drain the tank."

I gotta pee like a racehorse.
J'ai une putain d'envie de pisser.

I peed my pants.
Je me suis pissé dessus.

Chapter 5

Nice & Naughty
Sympa & Salace

The French have the reputation of being amazing lovers. Fact is, they're no physically better equipped to have sex than the rest of us. They just have more of it. Between their cushy 35-hour workweeks and five weeks of vacation a year, they simply have more time to fuck. Throw in their wine-fueled libertinism, and it's a minor miracle France doesn't have a population the size of China's.

Fucking
La baise

Tonight, I wanna....
Ce soir, je veux....

Let's go....
Allons....

You make me want to....
Tu me donnes envie de....

> **make love**
> *faire l'amour*
>
> **sleep with you**
> *coucher avec toi*
> *Coucher avec* is literally "to bed with." *Dormir avec*—"to sleep with"—is just for catchin' Z's.

fuck
baiser; niquer
From *forniquer.*

get off
tirer un coup
Literally, "to take a shot."

screw
tringler; troncher

get my rocks off
prendre mon pied
Literally, "to take my foot."

put it in your box
enfourner mon pain
Literally, "put my baguette in the oven."

stuff you
te bourrer

do the beast with two backs
faire la bête à deux dos

fuck you in the ass
t'enculer

fuck like rabbits
baiser comme des lapins

do it woman on top
s'empaler la foufoune
Literally, "impale the muff."

have a quickie
tirer un coup rapidos

He/She is down to fuck.
Il/Elle a le feu au cul.

He/She loves the dick.
C'est un cul à bites.
Literally, "He/She has an ass for dicks."

Positions, etc.
Les positions, etc.

If you want to learn the best and most innovative positions ever made in France, check out skin-flicks with Gallic studs like H.P.G. (Henri-Pierre Gustave), who claimed a length of 20 centimeters—which is metric for "huge." But mere mortals can thank a French production company which recently struck it rich through a retro approach for audiences tired of San Fernando Valley's absurd silicon-filled, mascara-covered bodies: "Jacquie et Michel" feature low budget, amateur-style home videos of ordinary folks gettin' their freak on. Their trademark consists of the actors randomly pausing in mid-action for an exchange addressed directly to the camera: "*Merci qui?*" "*Merci, Jacquie et Michel!*" ("Who should you thank?" "'Thank you,' Jacquie and Michel!"). It's one of the best-known sayings of the last few years in the French-speaking world.

Let's do....
Faisons....

Wanna try...?
Veux-tu essayer...?

How 'bout...?
Et si on faisait... ?

I'm tired of....
J'en ai marre de....

> **missionary style**
> *la position du missionnaire*
>
> **doggy style**
> *l'amour en levrette; à quatre pattes*
>
> **double penetration**
> *la double pénétration*
>
> **anal sex**
> *le sexe anal*

threesome
plan cul à trois
What the '70s called a *ménage à trois*; literally, a "three-person household."

foursome/fivesome/etc.
le plan baise à quatre/cinq/etc.

group sex
la partouze

Two to lift her, three to fill her.
Deux qui la tiennent, trois qui la pinent.
You know, the old porn cliché where two men hold the woman aloft and three others fill the usual orifices?

Take me **from behind** and cum in my ass.
*Prends-moi **par derrière** et jouis dans mon cul.*

The family jewels
Les bijoux de famille

Pénis for "penis," *vagin* for "vagina," and *anus* for "anus" are straightforward enough. But, after that, the French could fill a small dictionary with all their words for genitals. Sort of stands to reason that you'll have a lot of words for something when people are always talking about it.

Suck my...
Suce-moi le/la...

Play with my...
Joue avec mon/ma...

      dick
      bite

      tubesteak
      vier
      Literally, "my eggplant."

dong
chibre

prick
dard

purple-headed monster
chauve à col roulé
Literally, "baldy in a turtleneck"—ever looked closely at an uncircumcised penis?

I really like your huge....
J'adore...géant(e).

Geneviève thinks your...is so cute.
Geneviève trouve....vraiment mignon(ne).

trouser snake
ta queue; ta pine
This means that, in French, "tail" (*la queue*) refers to men, not women.

wood
ton gourdin
Literally, "a cudgel."

rod
ta verge; ta trique

tool
ton engin

the head
ton gland

wiener
ta saucisse

pecker
ta quéquette; ton zob

wee-wee
ton zizi; ta zézette

weenie
ta zigounette

COCK PARTY
FESTIVAL DE BITES

Dicks come—as it were—in all shapes and sizes.

A big dick
Une grosse bite; un braquemard
Le braquemard was a two-headed
club used in medieval battles.

A tiny dick
Une petite bite

A limp dick
Une bite molle

A half-boner
Un bande-mou

Hung like a horse
Monté comme un âne

> **wang**
> *ton zguègue; ton zboub*
> You probably don't know why it's called a "wang." We have no friggin' idea
> why the French call it *un zguègue.*

Tickle my....
Chatouille-moi....

Gargle my....
Gargarise-moi....

Massage my....
Masse-moi....

Can I shave your...?
Je peux te raser...?

> **balls**
> *les coquilles; les roustons; les burnes; les coucougnettes; les
> baloches*
>
> **nuts**
> *les bonbons*
>
> **scrotum**
> *le scrotum*
>
> **nutsack**
> *la bourse*
> Literally, "the spare-change purse."

package
le paquet

nards, nads
les roupettes; les roubignoles

Is your **nutsack** always that droopy?
*T'as toujours la **bourse** qui pend comme ça?*

....

Boobs
Lolos

I love....
J'adore....

Pinch my....
Pince-moi....

Can I squeeze your...?
Je peux te tripoter...?

> **tits**
> *les nichons; les nénés*

> **breasts**
> *les seins*

> **hooters**
> *les nibards*

> **boobs**
> *les lolos*

> **titties**
> *les tétés*

> **big tits**
> *les gros nichons*

> **huge tits**
> *les seins énormes*

You have great....
Tu as des...magnifiques.

> **torpedoes**
> *obus*

> **nipples**
> *mamelons*

> **nips**
> *tétons*

> **fake tits**
> *faux seins; nibards siliconés*

She's got no breasts.
*Elle a **pas de seins**.*

I'm as **flat as a cutting board.**
*Je suis **plate comme une planche à pain**.*

That's a huge rack!
Il y a du monde au balcon!
Literally, "There's a crowd on the balcony."

She's got the high beams on.
*Elle nous fait un appel de **phares**.*

....

Pussy
La chatte

Go down on my....
Va t'occuper de mon....

Be gentle with my....
Vas-y doucement avec mon....

> **vagina**
> *vagin*

> **pussy**
> *minou; minet*

cunt
con
Not nearly as harsh or vulgar as in English.

clitoris
clitoris

clit
clito; clitos

button
bouton

G-spot
point G

You have such a tight....
Ta...est vraiment étroite.

Your...is so wet.
Ta...est tellement mouillée.

I wanna finger your....
Je veux mettre le doigt dans ta....

pussy
chatte

snatch
motte

clam
moule

sweaty clam
moule qui suinte

slit
fente

vulva
vulve

Lick my....
Lèche-moi....

Eat my....
Bouffe-moi....

> **muff**
> *la touffe*
>
> **bush**
> *le gazon*
> Literally, "the lawn." And thus the term used by disappointed hetero men to designate lesbians: *gazon maudit* (lawn with a curse on it).
>
> **fur**
> *la fourrure*
>
> **beaver**
> *le hérisson*
> Literally, "hedgehog."
>
> **bearded clam**
> *le loutre*
> Literally, "otter."

I can't wait to go **muff-diving**.
J'ai hâte d'aller brouter du gazon.

I'm gonna **seriously stuff your pussy**.
Je vais t'en mettre plein la chatte.

I'm so horny, my **cunt is on fire**.
J'ai tellement envie, j'ai la chatte en feu.

Do you prefer **hairy** or **shaved** pussies?
Tu préfères les chattes touffues ou rasées?

My pussy is **dripping wet**.
J'ai la moule qui dégouline.

Damn, girl, **your pussy lips** taste so good.
Putain que j'adore le goût de tes lèvres.

That video's got some seriously **gaping pussies**.
Qu'est-ce qu'elle baille sérieusement de la chatte dans cette vidéo.

Ass
Cul

Anal sex is not as taboo in France, so you'll hear a lot of daily expressions using *enculer* (to ass-fuck or sodomize), including the metaphorical one, *enculer les mouches*, which literally means "to ass-fuck flies." It's used to describe someone who "nitpicks over ridiculously small details." Co-workers be warned.

Can I put it in your...?
Je peux le mettre dans ta/ton...?

Stick your fingers in my...
Mets tes doigts dans ma/mon...

Stroke my...
Caresse-moi la/le...

Grab my....
Attrape-moi le/la....

> **ass**
> *cul*
>
> **booty**
> *croupe*
>
> **asshole**
> *trou du cul*
>
> **buttcrack**
> *raie*
>
> **crack**
> *sourire vertical*
> Literally, "the vertical smile."
>
> **bunghole**
> *rondelle*
>
> **anus**
> *anus*

derriere
derrière

You have nice, strong **buns**.
*T'as des **miches** bien fermes et musclées.*

I want to lick you from your **hips** to your toes.
*Je veux te lécher des **hanches** jusqu'aux pieds.*

Let's ass-fuck without lubricant.
Enculons-nous à sec.

Sex fluids and pubic hair
Les liquides et les poils de l'amour

I've never seen so much/so many...in my life.
J'ai jamais vu tant de...de ma vie.

Can I eat/drink your...?
Je peux bouffer/boire ton/ta...?

Gross! I'm covered in....
Beurk! Je suis couvert de....

> **cum**
> *foutre*

> **semen**
> *sémence*

> **sperm**
> *sperme*

> **pussy juice**
> *crème de ta framboise*
> Literally, "cream off your raspberry."

> **female ejaculation**
> *éjaculation féminine*

> **short and curlies**
> *poils*

Shave my pussy.
Rase-moi la chatte.

When the river runs red, take the **Hershey trail**.
*Quand la rivière coule rouge, prends le **chemin boueux**.*
Literally, "the mud trail."

....

Foreplay
Les préliminaires

Sometimes it's not all about sex. Sometimes you gotta whisper a few sweet nothings into your lover's ear, give a little massage, and stop thinking about your own genitals for two seconds.

Can I...?
Je peux...?

> **kiss you**
> *t'embrasser*

> **suck you**
> *te sucer*

> **swallow you**
> *t'avaler*

Let's try...for a little while.
Tu veux essayer....

I'm tired of....
Je suis fatigué(e) de....

> **French-kissing**
> *rouler des pelles*

> **cuddling; hugging**
> *faire des câlins*

> **massaging your back**
> *te masser le dos*

SEX RHYMES
LES RIMES DU SEXE

The French are fond of making up little sex rhymes. The rhymes below aren't exactly up to Ludacris' standards, but they're still pretty fun in a dorky sort of way.

Women in glasses are crazy 'bout asses.
Femme à lunettes, femme à quéquettes.
Literally, "lady in glasses is crazy for dick."

Girls named Toni like it bony.
Martine, aime la pine.

Balls, Mrs. Rawls—your dog screws mine, and you say it's fine?
Mon vier Mme Olivier, votre chien encule le mien et vous dites que c'est rien?

trying to undo your fly
essayer d'ouvrir ta braguette

dry-humping
jouer à frotti-frotta
Literally, "playing rub-a-dub-dub."

finger-fucking
te doigter

fucking lube-free
limer à sec

Have you ever...?
As-tu déjà...?

been in an orgy
participé à une orgie

organized a free-for-all
organisé une partouze

been sandwiched
pris en sandwich

done a skin flick
tourné dans un film de cul

Fuck me with the **dildo**.
*Prends-moi avec un **godemichet**; un **gode**.*

Do you have a **vibrator**?
*Tu as un **vibromasseur**; un **vibro**?*

....

Oral sex
Le sexe oral

You know the old baseball analogy where first base means making out and a home run is sex? In the U.S., a lot of people will hand out the first few bases like free candy, but hold on to the home run ball for someone special. It's a little different in France. There, you're more likely to have sex than get a blow job or be eaten out, since oral sex is reserved for only the most intimate of couples. And swallowing after oral sex is even rarer still, because French girls *really* don't go for that.

I **suck** but I don't **swallow**.
*Je **suce** mais j'**avale** pas.*
This is a pretty common way for French girls to announce the rules in a straightforward manner.

Can I **sit on your face**?
*Puis-je **poser mon cul sur ta gueule**?*

How 'bout I **play the skin flute**?
*Je te **taille une pipe**?*
Literally, "whittling a wood pipe."

How 'bout a/some...?
Ça te dit...?

Have you ever tried...?
T'as déjà essayé...?

Let's switch it up and try....
Changeons un peu et essayons....

Let's film ourselves doing....
Filmons-nous en train de faire....

> **fellatio**
> *une fellation*

> **blow-job**
> *une turlute; un pompier; une pipe*

> **deep throat**
> *une gorge profonde*

> **cunnilingus**
> *le cunnilingus*

> **rim job**
> *la feuille de rose*
> Literally, "the pink leaf."

> **69**
> *le soixante-neuf*

> **titty-fucking**
> *la branlette espagnole*
> Literally, "a Spanish hand job."

> **bondage/S&M**
> *le bondage/S&M*

> **anal penetration**
> *la pénétration anale*

> **sodomy**
> *la sodomie*

> **an enema**
> *un lavement*

> **a facial**
> *l'éjac' faciale*

I'm coming!
Je jouis!

Grab some rubbers and memorize this section, because the only thing worse than not having a condom when you want to screw would be having to thumb through this chapter in the heat of the moment just to figure out how to tell your lover *Je jouis! Je jouis! Je jouis!*

I really like that!
J'aime beaucoup ça!

That's great!
C'est vraiment bon!

Are you getting hot?
Ça t'excite?

I'm totally drenched.
Je mouille comme une folle.
Literally, "I'm as wet as a crazy lady."

Damn, girl, I'm **getting hard**.
*Oh putain, je **commence à bander**.*

Do you have a **condom**?
*Tu as un **préservatif**?*

Do it.../I want it...
Fais-le.../Je le veux...

> **faster**
> *plus vite*
>
> **slower**
> *moins vite*
>
> **harder**
> *plus fort*
>
> **softer**
> *moins fort*

again
encore

again
encore

again
encore

Oh shit! I **busted the rubber.**
*Merde! J'ai **explosé la capote**.*
Le capot is the hood of a car, i.e., it covers the engine.

Can I cum…?
Je peux jouir…?

> **in your mouth**
> *dans ta bouche*

> **in your ass**
> *dans ton cul*

> **in your hand**
> *dans ta main*

> **on your face**
> *sur ton visage*

> **on your tits**
> *sur tes nichons*

I want **to cum.**
*Je veux **jouir**.*

I'm about to cum.
Je suis sur le point de jouir.

I'm coming!
Je jouis!

I'm gonna….
Je vais….

> **ejaculate**
> *éjaculer*

shoot my load
lâcher la marchandise

blow my wad
envoyer la purée

bust my nut
balancer la sauce

squirt
gicler

let go
décharger

Do you masturbate?
Tu te masturbes?

I **jack off** twice a day.
*Je **me branle** deux fois par jour.*

Go milk your rod.
Va faire pleurer le colosse.
Literally, "go make the giant cry."

Last night I had a **wet dream**.
*Hier soir j'ai eu une **émission nocturne**.*

Premature ejaculation is a bitch.
***L'éjaculation précoce** me casse les couilles.*

....

Sex fiends
Obsédé(e)s sexuel(le)s

Some people are defined by their job. Fluffers, for instance, are hired crew members whose job it is to keep male porn stars erect while they're off-camera getting ready for the next gang bang. Though you might not suck porn star dick for a living (not that there's anything wrong with that), chances are you've been defined by your sex life at one time or another.

My French boyfriend is...
Mon copain français est...

My American girlfriend is...
Ma copine américaine est...

Your ex sounds like...
Ton ex a l'air d'être...

Your mom is...
Ta mère est...

> **a sex fiend**
> *un(e) obsédé(e) sexuel(le)*
>
> **a nymphomaniac**
> *un(e) nymphomane*
>
> **a horndog**
> *un queuetard*
>
> **a slut**
> *une salope*
>
> **a skank**
> *une grognasse*
>
> **a walking sperm bank**
> *un garage à bites*
> Literally, "a parking garage for dicks."
>
> **a good fuck**
> *un bon coup*
>
> **a lousy lay**
> *un mauvais coup*
>
> **a virgin**
> *une vierge; un puceau; une pucelle*
>
> **a sadist**
> *un(e) sadique*
>
> **a masochist**
> *un(e) masochiste*

sado-masochist
un sado-maso

If she's gonna lie there like a dead fish, she's sleeping in the **wet spot** tonight.
*Si elle va rester là à faire **l'étoile de mer**, normal qu'elle dorme sur **la tâche mouillée**.*

Instead of "dead fish," the French say "starfish" because starfish have spread-open legs and never move.

Bad shit
Des trucs tordus

French is the language of love and poetry, of passion and romance. An exceptionally lyrical language, it is intellectual and existential, sensual and sensitive, as evidenced in these genteel phrases.

That whore gave me....
Cette pute m'a donné/m'a filé....

That asshole gave me....
Cet enculé m'a donné/m'a filé....

> **crabs**
> *les morpions*
>
> **herpes**
> *l' herpès*
>
> **AIDS**
> *le SIDA (le syndrome d'immunodéficience acquise)*
>
> **HIV**
> *le VIH (le virus de l'immunodéficience humaine)*
>
> **an STD**
> *une MST (une maladie sexuellement transmise)*

It's the first time I've had....
C'est la première fois que j'ai....

> **blue balls**
> *des couilles molles*

> **numb dick**
> *la bite engourdie*

> **drippy dick**
> *le robinet qui coule*

> **raw vag**
> *la chatte déchiquetée*

It **burns** when I **pee**.
*Ça **brûle** quand je **pisse**.*

CHAPTER 6

Smack Talk

Joutes verbales

Remember the 2006 World Cup, when Zidane head-butted that Italian sissy for calling his sister a whore? That was awesome! And not very representative of French culture. Like wannabe-rappers, your typical Frenchman will usually pose like a badass and make a lot of noise, but never actually throw down. This truism falls flat, though, when you enter the French ghettos on the outskirts of major cities, where about 100 cars are set on fire every weekend. So if you're into self-mutilation and internal bleeding, check it out! For the rest of us, there's deep breathing, counting to 10, and talking about our feelings.

Pissed off
Pétage de plombs

Skinny French people....
Des Français maigrichons....

Fat tourists....
Des gros porcs de touristes....

Euro hipsters....
Les bobos....

> **are too much**
> *me gavent*

get on my nerves
m'énervent

irritate the shit out of me
m'emmerdent

tick me off
me gonflent

wear me out
me saoulent

think they're the shit
se prennent pour le trou du cul de la planète
Literally, "the planet's bunghole."

don't give a shit about anybody else
s'en foutent des autres

I can't....
Je peux pas....

stand you
te supporter

put up with them
les encadrer

stand the sight of him/her
le/la voir

You are....
Tu es....

so full of shit
complètement faux cul

out of control
complètement givré(e)

totally crazy
complètement ouf

a pain in the ass
chiant(e)

a wimp
une lopette

wacked out
cinglé(e); fêlé(e)

totally clueless
un gros boloss

a buzzkill
lourd

creepy
chelou

Stop...
Arrête...

    busting our balls
    de nous casser les couilles

    talkin' shit about me
    *de **raconter des saloperies** sur mon compte*

    talkin' smack **behind my back**
    *de raconter des trucs **dans mon dos***

    goin' through my phone
    de fouiller dans mon portable

    lying like a rug
    *de **mentir** comme tu respires*
    Literally, "lying like you breathe."

    spouting bullshit
    de raconter n'importe quoi

He/She....
Il/Elle....

    looks like a real asshole
    a une vraie tête de con

    is bad news
    a mauvais caractère

looks pissed
a l'air fou furieux

could kill you with one look
a des couteaux à la place des yeux

stabbed me in the back
m'a poignardé dans le dos

stood me up
m'a posé un lapin
Literally, "left me a rabbit."

Assholes
Enculé(e)s

Thanks to globalization, certain types of people now suck all over the world.

Boss
Le patron; le boss; le chef

> **My boss** is a first-rate asshole.
> *Mon chef est un enculé de première.*

My ex
Mon ex

> **My ex** was a cheap-ass.
> *Mon ex était un gros radin.*

Lawyer
Un(e) avocat(e)

> To cheer me up, tell me some dead **lawyer** jokes.
> *Raconte-moi quelques blagues sur les **avocats**, histoire de me remonter le moral.*

Politician
Un homme/une femme politique

Never go with **a politician** into an airport bathroom.
*Ne va jamais dans les chiottes de l'aéroport avec **un homme politique**.*

Stepmom
Belle-mère

My stepmom confiscated my bong.
*Ma **belle-mère** m'a confisqué la pipe à eau.*

Father-in-law
Beau-père

Your father-in-law is kind of a hard-ass, isn't he?
*Ton **beau-père**, c'est pas un peu un dur à cuire?*

Jock
Un sportif/une sportive

The **jocks** at my school are dumb as a box a' rocks.
*Plus cons que les **sportifs** de ma fac, tu meurs.*
"Any dumber than the jocks at my school and you wouldn't be breathing."

He's/She's a...
C'est un/une...

bastard
connard/connasse

thug
voyou

asshole
salaud

bitch
salope; chienne

skanky slut
grosse pouffiasse

motherfucker
enculé(e)
Literally, "ass-fucked."

jerk
enfoiré(e)

loser
cake

dickhead
tête de vier

....

The man with the badge
Les forces de l'ordre

On the list of people who are always there when you don't
need them, cops deserve a special place. The French have a
regular police force (*la police*) just like in the U.S. But they also
have the *gendarmes*, a national police squad used mostly in the
countryside, who are a bit like the hick cops in old *Starsky and
Hutch* episodes. If you're thinking about smoking out in public,
keep in mind that the B.A.C. (*la Brigade anti-criminalité*) circulates
in unmarked cars. And then there's the C.R.S. (*les Compagnies
républicaines de sécurité*), the riot police, which are a combination
of national guard and SWAT team nicknamed *les Playmobils*—
these are the real badasses. When the shit goes down in Paris, the
government sends out busloads of these guys packing helmets,
masks, shoulder and knee pads, boots, batons, shields, and tear
gas. Use one of the following phrases right before they blast you in
the face with pepper spray.

Watch out, here come **the cops**!
*Vingt-deux, v'là **les flics**.*
There are lots of explanations for the *vingt-deux* (22), but no one knows for sure.

Fucking cops.
Enculés de flics.

The men in blue
Les petits hommes bleus

The pigs
Les poulets
In the U.S., when the cops are around, "Smells like bacon!"; in France, it's chicken (*les poulets*).

> Let's go. **Smells like bacon** around here.
> *On se casse. **Ça sent les poulets** par ici.*

The narcs
La brigade des stups
Short for *stupéfiants*, "stupefying," in the sense of intoxicating

The police wagon
Le panier à salade
Literally, "the salad basket," from the boxes used to ship heads of lettuce.

A motorcycle cop
Un motard

A K9 cop
Un maître chien

The **dog** is taking his cop for a walk.
*C'est le **chien** qui le tient en laisse.*

A meter maid
Un pigeon
Because of the snazzy powder-blue hat and pantsuit they wear.

Why don't you **arrest** some real criminals instead of sticking me with a **parking ticket**?
*Vous feriez mieux **d'arrêter** de vrais criminels au lieu de me coller un **PV**!*

Watch it, this town is full of **speed traps**!
*Faites gaffe, ce bled est bourré de **radars**!*

Fuck the police!
Nique la police!

Getting arrested
Se faire tauler

Remember, *délater, tu te fais latter* (snitches get stitches). So if the pigs pick you up, you didn't see shit. Ya heard?

I won't say a word without my lawyer.
Je dirais rien sans un avocat.

It wasn't me.
C'est pas moi.

I don't know anything.
Je sais rien.

Act like you don't know shit.
Fais comme si de rien n'était.

Fighting words
Ça va filer

To get a sense of how violent some of the bad neighborhoods in France are, rent *La Haine* ("Hate") by Mathieu Kassovitz, France's answer to Quentin Tarantino. It takes place in the housing projects and starts with awesome battle scenes between the project dwellers and the C.R.S. After you get all juiced up on adrenaline, master the following phrases, grab your brass knuckles, and join in the fray.

I hate you.
Je te déteste.

Get lost.
Fous le camp.

Don't make me blow a fuse/burst a vein!
Ne me fais pas péter les plombs/péter une durite!

Scram.
Dégage.

Go to hell.
Va te faire voir.

Leave me the hell alone.
Fous-moi la paix.

Man up!
Assume, quoi!

You looking for a fight?
Tu cherches la baston?

Fuck off.
Va te faire foutre.
Literally, "Go make yourself come."

You're so **lame** at video games!
T'es une vraie quiche aux jeux vidéo!

He's a total **bummer**.
Il est complètement nase.

Chicken shit!
Couille molle!
Literally, "soft in the balls."

Sometimes things suck so bad, you're a little bit of everything. For those times where you're halfway between "bummed" and "really pissed," there's *le seum*:

I'm totally bummed-pissed!
J'ai trop le seum!

More shit talk
Toujours grande gueule

Most French shit talking isn't that different from what we say in the States when we're fed up with someone's bullshit.

What did you just **say**!?!
*Qu'est-ce t'as **dit** là!?!*

You wanna **say that again**?
Répète un peu pour voir?

Shut your face.
Ferme ta gueule; Ferme-la.

Shut the fuck up.
Ferme ta clape-merde.
Literally, "Shut your shit-mouth."

You're worthless.
T'es un moins que rien.

You got a **problem**?
*T'as un **problème**?*

Watch your ass!
Gare ta gueule!

Let's take it **outside**.
*Je t'attends **dehors**.*

I'll **fix** your ass.
*Je vais **te mettre** ton compte.*

I'll have your **hide**.
*J'aurai ta **peau**.*

I'll wipe the floor with you.
Je te mettrai minable.

You're gonna eat **dirt**.
*Tu vas manger le **bitume**.*

They're gonna **throw down**.
*Ça va **filer**!*

I got in a **fight** last night.
*Je me suis **battu** hier soir.*

Damn, they pounded the shit out of each other!
Putain, qu'est-ce qu'ils se sont mis!

Are there a lot of **bar brawls** in France?
*Est-ce qu'il y a beaucoup de **filades dans les bars** en France?*

Punches and kicks
Coups de poings et coups de pieds

To hit somebody
Frapper quelqu'un

To slap somebody
Gifler quelqu'un

To nail somebody
Choper quelqu'un

To smack somebody
Donner une baffe à quelqu'un

A **strong punch**
*Une **patate***
Literally, "potato."

To kick someone in....
Mettre un coup de pied dans....

> **the head**
> *la tête*
>
> **the stomach**
> *le ventre*
>
> **the butt**
> *le cul*
>
> **the balls**
> *les couilles*

To pound with your fist
*Mettre un **coup de poing***

To **head-butt**
*Donner un **coup de tête/coup de boule***
Coupe de boule means to hit with the "bowling ball."

A bloody nose
Saigner du nez

A black eye
Un œil au beurre noir
Literally, "an eye with black butter."

He **busted** that guy's nose.
Il lui a cassé le nez au mec.

Yo! **Mud wrestling**, I'm all over that!
Oh! Les combats dans la boue, j'adore ça!

It's all in the family?
Tout pour la famille?

France isn't nearly as PC as the United States, so race talk gets people riled up, but not as much as it does in the States. Instead of race, anything with "mother" in it is gonna get French dudes really pissed off. It's a Catholic country, goddammit! What the motherfuck do you expect?

Fuck your race.
Nique ta race.
"Race" is used loosely, to mean your "tribe" or "people." Along the same lines, turf wars and housing project posturing lead to insults about "your dead" (*tes morts*), that is, your ancestry.

Fuck your ancestors!
Enculé de tes morts!

You typical ethnic bastard.
Enculé de ta race.
Literally means "assfuck of your race" but loosely translates to "you're just like every other white/black/Latino/etc. bastard."

Motherfucker
Enculé de ta mère

Fuck your mother.
Nique ta mère.

THE ART OF THE FRENCH INSULT
L'ART DE L'INSULTE À LA FRANÇAISE

The word *con* is used to say just about everything in French slang. It comes from the same word as "cunt," but doesn't have that word's harshness. It's much closer to "jerk" or "ass." The French combine it with various adjectives to give it different meanings.

Un con
An ass

Un pauvre con
A pathetic loser

Un petit con
A sneaky jerk

Un gros con
A screaming asshole

Un brave con
A loser with a good heart

Your mother's a whore.
Ta mère la pute.

Son-of-a-bitch
Fils de pute

Your mother gave birth in a trash can.
Ta mère elle a accouché dans une poubelle.
A classic French middle school insult

Your momma works at Sam's Club.
Ta mère elle travaille à Monoprix.
Monoprix is the French equivalent of the U.S. superstore.

Yeah, well, your momma wears a thong on TV.
Ta mère en string à la télé.

The peacemaker
Le pacifiste

Mellowed out, Owen Wilson–style surfer types *do* exist in the southwest of France. On the Mediterranean coast, they're more into windsurfing (*planche à voile*) and energy drinks, while out in the countryside they're pot-smoking vegetarians who gave up their Mercedes in the city to commune with nature. But deep down inside, they all want everyone to just get along.

Yo, dude, it's all right, chill out.
Ça va, mec, c'est bon, calme-toi.

Don't get all worked up.
Te monte pas le mou.

Don't get yourself in **such a state**.
Faut pas te mettre dans des états pareils.

That doesn't help a thing.
Ça sert à rien.

What's gotten into you?
Qu'est-ce qui t'as pris?

Take a **deep breath**.
Respire un bon coup.

I'm just a **laid-back guy**.
Je suis un calme.

I don't like getting **involved**.
J'aime pas les embrouilles.

Forget about it.
Laisse tomber.

Don't let yourself get pissed over that.
Te prends pas la tête pour ça.

Don't let it get to you.
Te prends pas le chou.

Get over it.
Tourne la page.

Who gives a shit!?
Qu'est-ce qu'on s'en bat les couilles!?

Knock it off.
Arrête tes conneries.

Call an ambulance.
Appelle le SAMU. (Service d'Aide Médicale Urgente)

Call the cops.
Appelle les flics.

CHAPTER 7

Pop Culture & Technology
Culture Pop & Technologie

....

Movies
Le cinéma

France has the third-largest film industry in the world (behind India and the United States). If it weren't for France we wouldn't even *have* movies, since it was two French brothers, Auguste and Louis Lumière, who invented the film camera. A lot of French movie genres parallel the English: *un film d'action, un film d'horreur, un film romantique, un film de science fiction,* and so on. If you hate *les comédies musicales* as much as we do, you can always lie to your friends and claim this book says they don't exist in France.

Wanna catch **a movie**?
*On se regarde **un film**?*

Wanna go see a **flick**?
*On va au **cinoche**?*

How 'bout a...?
Ça te dirait...?

> **cartoon**
> *un dessin animé*

tearjerker
un film à l'eau de rose

Lifetime-original movie
un film cucul la praline

chick flick
un film pour les gonzesses

dubbed movie
un film doublé; un film en v.f. (en version française)
Except in Paris, foreign films in theaters and on TV are usually dubbed.

skin flick
un film de cul

movie with subtitles
un film en v.o. (en version originale)
I.e., in its original language with subtitles

Let's see it on the **big screen**.
*On se le mate sur **grand écran**.*

Get me a **ticket**.
*Donnez-moi une **place**.*

Hey! **The line** starts back there!
*Oh! **La queue** c'est là-bas derrière qu'elle commence!*

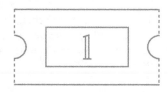

Dwayne Johnson sounds stupid even when he's **dubbed**!
*Dwayne Johnson a l'air abruti même **en v.f.**!*

Kick the back of my chair one more time and I'll stuff that **popcorn** through your face.
*Tu me mets encore un coup de pied dans le fauteuil et les **pop-corn** je te les rentre par le nez!*

FEMALE FRENCH STARS
VEDETTES FRANÇAISES

French actresses have captivated audiences for decades. Here are a few of the current *femmes* turning heads.

The adorable face of *Amélie*, Audrey Tautou was chosen as the French actress for *The Da Vinci Code*. French folks love her or despise her.

Unlike Tautou, Marion Cotillard has had some success in Hollywood, and even won an Academy Award for best actress. But what she is really known for is having allegedly contributed to the breakup of Brangelina.

Finally, Léa Seydoux and Adèle Exarchopoulo, co-stars of *Blue Is the Warmest Color*, make both Tautou and Cotillard look like has-been whiners. Check out their respective PornHub pages to get the full, err, perspective.

I'm tired of these **lame-ass movies**.
*J'en ai marre de ces **films bouffe-couilles**.*
Literally, "movies that eat your balls."

Dude! They show **porn** on French TV!
*Hé mec! Ils passent des **films de cul** à la télé française!*
The French premium channel Canal+ (similar to HBO) features a new porn film every first Saturday of the month.

Music
La musique

Did you know that the Stade de France soccer stadium outside Paris is one of the biggest concert venues in Europe? Or that France is the second-largest market for rap in the world, behind the U.S.? Inspired by the great groundbreakers MC Solaar, Suprême NTM, and IAM, a new generation of French rappers is making a name for itself. Check out Booba, Rhoff, Jul, Alonzo, PNL, and

Soprano. That said, do not show up dressed in a Booba t-shirt at the Rhoff's concert and vice versa! You have been warned!

I can't stand that....
Je peux pas supporter....

I'm in love with that....
J'adore....

> **musician**
> *ce/cette musicien(ne)*
>
> **lead singer**
> *ce chanteur/cette chanteuse*
>
> **drummer**
> *ce batteur/cette batteuse*
>
> **bassist**
> *ce/cette bassiste*
>
> **guitar player**
> *ce/cette guitariste*
>
> **album**
> *ce disque*
>
> **song**
> *cette chanson*
>
> **cover song**
> *cette reprise*
>
> **video**
> *cette vidéo*
>
> **DJ**
> *ce/cette dj*
> Pronounced "dee-gee."

Where can we catch...?
Où peut-on écouter...?

> **some good tunes** around here
> ***de la bonne 'zique*** *par ici*

some **live music** in this town
*de la **musique en direct** dans ce bled*

a good concert
un bon concert

I'm with the **band**.
*Je fais partie du **groupe**.*

I'm totally into **rap**.
*Je kiffe grave le **rap**.*

I play my **tunes** loud!
*J'écoute la **'zique** à fond!*

Girl drummers are hot.
*Les **batteurs-filles** sont bandantes.*

My roommate **sings** Stromae in the shower.
*Mon camarade de chambre **chante** Stromae dans la douche.*

Crank it!
Monte le son!

TUNES
'ZIQUE

Most styles of current music come from the U.S., so the names are
the same in French: *le rock, le rap, le hip-hop, le funk, la soul, le R 'n'
B, la country, la pop, le jazz, la musique classique, le reggae, le ska, la
world*. The sub-genres of EDM, all very popular in France, follow suit
as well: *la disco, la techno, l'électro*, etc. Exceptions? *La variété* is code
for Céline Dion–soundalikes, and *la trad'* is the French version of
neofolk (music from Brittany or Corsica, for instance, that use regional
instruments made from sheep guts and declaimed in Bono-style
indecipherable local dialects).

Comics
La BD

Graphic novels are considered an art form and have an illustrious history in France. In any French bookstore, you'll find a comics section where adults and kids alike sit and read for hours. *Les Aventures de Tintin* and *Astérix* of generations past have new rivals in popular series such as *Largo Winch* (the worlds of high finance and criminal intrigue collide), *Le Combat ordinaire* (a war photographer tries to recover from the horrors seen), and Enki Bilal's futurist *Nikopol Triology*. Bringing hardcore humor to the masses are *Le Gros Dégueulasse* ("Filthy, Disgusting Bastard," written and drawn by Reiser) and *Maurice et Patapon* (by Charb, the cartoonist and editor-in-chief of *Charlie Hebdo*, assassinated by terrorists in 2015). For more literary tastes, Joann Sfar's tales of 1930s Algeria, Blain & Lanzac's spoofs of French diplomacy, and Riad Sattouf's reflections of his childhood in the Middle East are available in English (as *The Rabbi's Cat*, *Weapons of Mass Diplomacy*, and *The Arab of the Future*, respectively).

Do you have any...?
Avez-vous...?

> **comic books**
> *des bandes dessinées*
>
> **comics**
> *des BD*
>
> **new editions**
> *des nouvelles éditions*
>
> **first editions**
> *des premières éditions*

Who's your favorite...?
Qui est ton...?

> **superhero**
> *super héros favori*
>
> **villain**
> *méchant préféré*
>
> **sidekick**
> *frère d'armes préféré*
>
> **mutant**
> *mutant favori*
>
> **monster**
> *monstre préféré*
>
> **nefarious evildoer**
> *scélérat néfaste favori*

Here are some of the classics:

Les Aventures de Tintin et Milou
The Adventures of Tintin and Milou

Written and drawn by the Belgian Hergé, this is probably the most famous French-language comic of all time. It tells of Tintin, a young reporter, and his dog Milou who travel around the world and even to the moon to solve mysteries.

Les Aventures d'Astérix le Gaulois
Asterix the Gaul

A close second in international popularity is *Asterix the Gaul*, written by René Goscinny and drawn by the Belgian Albert Uderzo. These patriotic tales tell the story of a small Gallic village in Brittany, led by the mustachioed hero Asterix, who resists the Roman Invasion thanks to powers acquired by drinking a magical potion. Asterix was no surrender monkey!

Le Petit Nicolas
Little Nicholas

These hugely popular kids' stories, originally published in the early '60s, were also written by René Goscinny and were illustrated by Jean-

Jacques Sempé, from the perspective of Little Nicholas himself and showing his child's-eye view of the world. His naive perceptions often reveal themselves to be truer than those of the adults around him.

Fashion
La mode

Fashion is another area where the French set the international standard. Many of the greatest designers and brands, past and present, come from France: Louis Vuitton, Coco Chanel, Christian Dior, Pierre Cardin, Guess, Lacoste. While it may be cool in the U.S. to show up looking like you just dragged your ass out of bed, that shit won't fly in France.

I love your **outfit**!
*J'adore ta **tenue**!*

You've got a great **look**.
*J'adore ton **look**.*

I don't like her/his **walk**.
*J'aime pas sa **dégaine**.*

You're totally sexy **in that**.
*T'es super sexy **comme ça**.*

I can't believe he's wearing that!
Il est putain de mal fringué, je le crois pas!

You fucked up my **favorite shirt**!
*Tu m'as salopé ma **chemise préférée**!*

Go put on a/some....
Va te mettre un/une/des....

Take off that/those....
Enlève ce/cette/ces....

> **dirty clothes**
> *fringues dégueulasses*

dress clothes
tenue de soirée

tuxedo
smoking

evening gown
robe de soirée

suit
costard

pants
falzar

kicks (shoes)
godasses

sunglasses
lunettes de soleil

Nice **threads**!
*Belles **fringues**!*

Babe, you've got swag.
Tu as le swag, bébé.

THE LAST LAYER
LA DERNIÈRE ÉTOFFE

Tighty-whities
Un slip kangourou

Boxers
Un caleçon

Underwear
Slip

Bra
Un soutien-gorge; un sous-tifs

Panties
Une culotte

Thong
Un string

Speedo
Un slip de bain
What Brits and Australians so elegantly call "a Budgie smuggler" is known as a *moule-bite* (dick-hugger) on the beaches of Nice and Saint Tropez.

Bikini
Un bikini

You're lookin' all....
T'as l'air très....

> **in fashion**
> *à la mode*
>
> **well-dressed**
> *bien sapé(e)*
>
> **badly dressed**
> *mal sapé(e)*
>
> **trendy**
> *tendance*
>
> **preppy**
> *BCBG*
> Short for *Bon Chic Bon Genre* (right style, right brand)

....

Money
L'argent

Most of the good things in life cost money. And, in France, those good things cost twice as much money.

Cash
Blé
Literally, "wheat."

Coins
De la monnaie

Bucks
Balles

Dough
Pognon

Bills
Billets

Big money
Thune
This refers to someone who has, or is, Big Money.

Can you give me change, please?
Vous pouvez me faire la monnaie, s'il vous plaît?

You can keep the change.
Vous pouvez garder la monnaie.

I'm totally broke!
J'ai pas un rond!

The media
Les médias

From print to radio to television, here's everything you need to know about French media.

NEWSPAPERS
LES JOURNAUX

Since France is smaller than the U.S. (roughly the size of Texas), newspapers tend to be national rather than regional. The four major papers are:

> *Le Monde:* No color pictures, no comics—just serious news.
> *Le Figaro:* The paper for wealthy conservatives.
> *Libération:* For hipsters and wannabes.
> *L'Equipe:* If *ESPN* were a daily newspaper...

While the first three are equivalent to the *New York Times* or the *Washington Post*, the fourth covers only sports and outsells all the others. They all struggle today, though, because of internet news and because in Paris you can get free newspapers at the métro.

MAGAZINES
LES MAGAZINES

Weekly news magazines *Le Point*, *L'Express*, and *Le Nouvel Observateur* match up with our *Time*, *Newsweek*, and *US News & World Report*. For the latest in music, film, TV, theater, art, and politics, give *Les Inrocks* a try (the full title, *Les Inrockuptibles*, is a play on "Les Incorruptibles").

To get the latest celeb news (*les infos people*) on who's sleeping with who, and to see pix of the latest nip slip, ask for *Gala*, *Voici*, or *Closer*, racier equivalents of *People* and *Us Weekly*. This fascination with celebrity gossip has been a recent discovery for the French, who, for the longest time, thought they didn't like that kind of thing, but are now obsessed with it.

Instead of the televised political satire of *The Daily Show*, John Oliver, and Steven Colbert, the French have two famous weekly papers, notorious for how often they have been censored (which in France takes the form of the government seizing the entire print run of an issue).

Le Canard enchaîné—the "duck in chains," with *canard* being slang for a newspaper—has set a standard for investigating corruption and uncovering scandals that makes the *Washington Post*'s Watergate coup look minor league in comparison.

Charlie Hebdo's brand of provocative cartooning (offset by thoughtful, progressive editorials) has a long history of pissing off France's reactionaries. Tragically, it more recently made them a target for Islamic terrorists, resulting in the massacre of 12 members of the staff and various security personnel on January 7, 2015. *Je suis Charlie* ("I am Charlie," we are all *Charlie Hebdo*) was the worldwide slogan that grew out of the outpouring of sympathy following the attack.

FRENCH TV
LA TÉLÉ

You can't escape trashy American TV merely by coming to France. Most popular American shows, and even some American rejects, run dubbed in French. Now you know why they hate us.

Let's watch....
Regardons....

...is my favorite show.
...est mon émission préférée.

Is...on?
Est-ce que...passe maintenant?

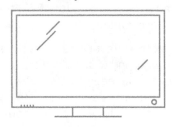

Game of Thrones
Le Trône de Fer
Literally, "The iron throne."

Arrested Development
Les Nouveaux Pauvres
Literally, "The new poor."

The Wire
Sur écoute
Literally, "Wire-tapped."

Many popular French reality shows (*émissions de téléréalité*) are content just to rip off a proven formula and appear as spin-offs *made in France*:

Survivor
Koh Lanta

Dancing with the Stars
Danse avec les Stars

Temptation Island
L'île de la tentation

American Idol
Nouvelle Star

This is the French version of *American Idol*, which is actually a spin-off of the original British show *Pop Idol*.

The Bachelor
Bachelor, le gentleman célibataire

Literally, "Bachelor, the unmarried gentleman."

Top Chef
Top Chef

Kitchen Nightmares
Cauchemar en cuisine

Literally, "Nightmare in the kitchen."

Gamers and techies
Joueurs et bidouilleurs

French youth have joined the nerd fest. But if the appeal of RPGs is universal, fortunately for traveling Americans, most of the terminology remains English in origin.

I'll kick your ass....
Je vais te mettre minable....

> **at video games**
> *aux jeux vidéo*

> **at Playstation**
> *à la Playstation*

> **at Xbox**
> *au 'box*

> **on the computer**
> *à l'ordinateur*

> **at Guitar Hero**
> *sur Guitar Hero*

Don't touch....
Ne touche pas....

Press....
Appuie sur....

>**the control**
>*les manettes de jeu*

>**the pause button**
>*le bouton de pause*

>**the trigger**
>*la gâchette*

>**the joystick**
>*le joystick*

>**the console**
>*la console*

You always press **reset** right when I'm about to destroy you.
*Tu appuies toujours sur le **bouton de remise à zero** quand je suis sur le point de te détruire.*

Download it to my....
Télécharge-le sur mon....

It's on my....
C'est sur mon....

>**cell phone/laptop**
>*portable*
>*Portable* is used for both cell phones and laptops.

>**tablet**
>*tablette*

>**MP3**
>*mp3*
>Pronounced "em-pay-twah."

>**program**
>*logiciel*

TEXT MESSAGING
TEXTER

Text messaging has led to whole new ways of writing things by abbreviation:

Hey	slt	*Salut*
Hey, you	cc	*Coucou*
Doin' alright?	cv?	*Ça va?*
What're you up to?	tfk	*Tu fais quoi?*
What's new?	Koi29	*Quoi de neuf?*
No worries	tkt	*T'inquiète*
Later	A+	*à plus*
Catch you later	A12C4	*À un de ces quatre*
LOL	mdr	*Mort de rire;* "dying laughing"
Hahaha!	Hihi!	
Damn	bdl	*Bordel*
Shit	ptn	*Putain*
Screw you	tg	*Ta gueule*
Shut your yap	Ftg	*Ferme ta gueule*
Kiss my ass	jtmd	*Je t'emmerde*
SOB	fdp	*Fils de pute*
Go fuck yourself	vtff	*Va te faire foutre*
Couldn't care less	blc	*(Je m'en) bats les couilles*
My ass	(.)	*Mon cul*
Hey, I'm just sayin'	jdcjdr	*Je dis ça, je dis rien*
FML	GlaN	*J'ai la haine;* "Fuck my life"

USB key drive
clé USB

hard drive
disque dur

I blew out my hard drive.
J'ai explosé mon disque dur.

We downloaded a shitload of MP3s.
On a téléchargé toute une flopée de mp3.

Send me an email.
Envoie-moi un email/un courriel.

Did you get my **text message**?
*T'as eu mon **texto**?*

Can I use your **phone charger**?
*Est-ce que je peux utiliser ton **chargeur**?*

What's the **password** for the Wi-Fi connection?
*C'est quoi, le **mot de passe**, pour la connexion Wi-Fi?*
Pronounced "wee-fee."

Do you have an American **keyboard**?
*Vous avez des **claviers** américains?*

Text me later.
Envoie-moi un texto/un SMS.

I'll text you.
Je t'envoie un mot.

They've still got **CD players** in their rent-a-wrecks!
*Ils ont toujours des **lecteurs CD** dans leurs voitures de location pourries!*

Chapter 8

Sports & Games
Sports & Jeux

Soccer is called "football" or just "foot" in France, and is far and away the most popular sport in the country. Nothing else even comes close. What's more, while French women never, ever used to play or watch soccer, les Bleues have racked up impressive performances against the U.S. national women's squad and have now joined their male counterparts as being among the top-ranked teams in the world. And though France might be a relatively small country, it can think large when it comes to sports: the Vendée Globe is a solo-unassisted, no-stops, around-the-world boat race. Other big sports are tennis, rugby, bicycling, judo, skiing, and Formula One racing, which is like a less-hicked-out version of NASCAR.

The essentials
Les essentiels

I play....
Je joue au....

Do you play...?
Est-ce que tu joues au...?

Wanna go play some...?
Tu veux jouer au...?

Let's see if there's any...on TV.
Voyons voir s'il y a du....à la télé.

> **soccer**
> *football; foot*
>
> **indoor soccer**
> *foot en salle*
>
> **tennis**
> *tennis*
>
> **golf**
> *golf*
>
> **basketball**
> *basket*
>
> **volleyball**
> *volley*
>
> **bowling**
> *bowling*
> Pronounced "BOO-ling."
>
> **football**
> *football américain*
>
> **baseball**
> *baseball*
>
> **hockey**
> *hockey sur glace*
>
> **rugby**
> *rugby*
>
> **bocce ball**
> *aux boules; à la pétanque*

Bowling is a sport for jackoffs.
Le bowling est un sport de branleurs.

The old-timers play **bocce ball** by the main square.
*Sur la place, les vieux jouent **aux boules/à la pétanque**.*

Live from the stadium
En direct du stade

If you get a chance to go to a soccer game in France, jump on it. The French national team plays in the Stade de France (in Saint-Denis, just north of Paris). The two most famous pro teams are Paris–St. Germain (PSG), whose home field is the Parc des Princes in southwest Paris, and Olympique de Marseille (OM), which does battle in the Stade Vélodrome down on the Mediterranean coast. The bitter rivalry between PSG and OM is similar to that of the Yankees and Red Sox—except that Red Sox fans don't fight it out with Yankees fans with bats and bricks at highway rest stops.

Let's go to....
Allons à....

> **a game**
> *un match*

> **a football game**
> *un match de foot*

> **a match**
> *une partie*

> **the championship game/the final**
> *la finale*

> **the tournament**
> *un tournoi*

> **the stadium**
> *au stade*

> **the field**
> *sur le terrain*

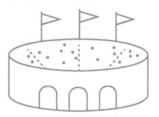

Check out....
Regarde....

>### the scoreboard
>*le tableau d'affichage*
>
>### the players
>*les joueurs*
>
>### the teams
>*les équipes*
>
>### the lineups
>*la compo pour le match*

Is it **halftime** yet?
*C'est bientôt la **mi-temps**?*

The Belgian **league** is terrible.
*Le **championnat** belge est nul.*

....

Other sports
D'autres sports

Skiing is a huge sport in France, especially in the Alps. But be prepared for total anarchy at the ski lifts. Orderly lines don't exist in France (this is also true of airports, bar counters, ticket lines, and the like). Be ready to bull your way through, and don't hesitate to put your skis on top of someone else's.

The French are great at....
Les Français sont très forts....

>### skiing
>*au ski*
>
>### biking
>*au vélo*
>
>### jogging
>*au footing*

skateboarding
au skate

gymnastics
à la gymnastique

track and field
à l'athlétisme

archery
au tir à l'arc

combat sports
aux sports de combat

martial arts
aux arts martiaux

boxing
à la boxe

judo
au judo

karate
au karaté

tae kwon do
au tae kwon do

waterskiing
au ski nautique

surfing
au surf

windsurfing
à la planche à voile

swimming
à la natation

wrestling
à la lutte

pro wrestling
au catch
This is like the fake WWE-style pro wrestling in the United States.

ATB or MTB
au VTT ("vélo tout terrain")

mountain climbing
à l'alpinisme

rock climbing
à l'escalade

scuba diving
à la plongée

rafting
au rafting

sportfishing
à la pêche au gros
Literally, "fishing for big ones."

skank fishing
à draguer les gros thons
Literally, "fishing for nasty tuna," i.e., hitting on uglies.

I can **break** three bricks with my hand.
*Je peux **casser** trois briques avec ma main.*

I'm a **black belt** in judo.
*Je suis **ceinture noire** de judo.*

The **gold-medal winner** is built like a Chinese swimmer.
*La **médaille d'or**, elle a le physique d'une nageuse chinoise.*

My team got its butt kicked on the **obstacle course**.
*Mon équipe en a pris plein la gueule dans **l'épreuve du raid.***

The fans
Les supporteurs

The United States believes in free enterprise, so heckling by the crowd is done on an individual basis. France believes in unions, so they have organized fan clubs in the stands, complete with microphones and memorized songs. Not only do they support the team by acting as the Twelfth Man and booing the opposing team—actually, they whistle in France—but they can even exert pressure in personnel decisions or force management to invest more money in the free-agent market. These people are rabid fanatics, even to the point of tragedy: Every year a few deaths occur in brawls between rival European clubs.

The stands
Les tribunes

The fans
Les supporteurs

Fan clubs
Les clubs de supporteurs

To bet
Parier
Betting on sports is legal in France. You can open an account online or fill out a ticket in a *bar-tabac*.

The referee
L'arbitre

Banner displays in the end zones
Les tifos

Where can I watch the game tonight?
Où puis-je voir le match ce soir?

Shit, the game's on a premium channel.
Merde, le match passe sur une chaîne payante.

Who's playing?
C'est qui contre qui?

What's the score?
Quel est le score?

Who scored?
Qui a marqué?

Wanna get a cold one at the half?
On se boit une mousse à la mi-temps?

You'll only get to use this if you watch the game at someone's house or in a bar; there's no booze allowed in French stadiums.

What an awesome goal!
Quel but magnifique!

That'll make the highlight reel!
C'est un but d'anthologie!

The ref robbed us!
On s'est fait voler par l'arbitre!

The ref is a fucking asshole.
L'arbitre est un gros enculé.

Our team's gonna cream you this year!
Notre équipe va vous laminer cette année!

We are the champions.
On est les champions.

Board and bar games
Sports de salon et de troquet

Sometimes you just don't feel like running much. In addition to the grueling efforts required by armchair quarterbacking, these games go down easy with pizza and beer.

Do I look like someone who can do crosswords?
J'ai une tête à faire des mots croisés?

Every time you do **sudokus** in the car, you end up puking.
*À chaque fois que tu fais des **sudoku** en bagnole, tu finis par gerber.*

Did you do that Mickey Mouse **jigsaw puzzle** all by yourself?
*Tu l'as fait tout seul ce **puzzle** de Mickey Mouse?*

Does "shithead" count in **Scrabble**?
*On compte ou pas "tête de con" au **Scrabble**?*
Pronounced "SCRA-bleuh."

I play **strip poker** just to flash my tats and piercings.
*Je joue au **strip-poker** rien que pour faire mater mes tatouages et mes piercing.*

Let's play....
Jouons....

> **board games**
> *à des jeux de société*
>
> **Monopoly**
> *au Monopoly; au Monop'*
>
> **chess**
> *aux échecs*
>
> **checkers**
> *au jeu de dames*
>
> **cards**
> *aux cartes*
>
> **Cards Against Humanity**
> *à Limite Limite*
>
> **Truth or Dare**
> *à Conséquence ou Vérité*
>
> **poker**
> *au poker*
>
> **rummy**
> *au rami*

> **bridge**
> *au bridge*

We suck at....
On est nuls au/aux....

> **pool**
> *billard*

> **darts**
> *fléchettes*

> **pinball**
> *flipper*

> **foosball**
> *baby foot*

Hitting the weights
Se mettre aux haltères

You won't see many fat people in France. In fact, "obese" by French standards doesn't even qualify for "overweight" in U.S. statistics.

I do....
Je fais....

> **some exercise**
> *de l'exercice*

> **some lifting**
> *de la muscu*

> **some weightlifting**
> *des haltères*

> **stationary riding**
> *du vélo de salon*

> **push-ups**
> *des pompes*

aerobics
de l'aérobic

yoga
du yoga

water boxing
de l'aqua-boxing

Zumba / Aqua Zumba
de la zumba / de l'aqua Zumba

The gym
Le gym

The weight room
La salle de muscu

The treadmill
Le tapis de course

The exercise mat
Le tapis de sol

The weights
Les haltères

I hit the **weight room** every day.
*Je vais à la **salle de muscu** tous les jours.*

Check out how **buff** he is.
*T'as vu comme il est **baraqué**.*

I got a ways to go before I get **washboard abs**.
*Pour les abdos, c'est pas encore des **tablettes de chocolat**.*
Literally, "chocolate bars."

Maybe we could **kick back** later in the Jacuzzi?
*On pourrait peut-être **se relaxer** après dans le Jacuzzi?*

The main events
Les grandes manifestations sportives

In France, March Madness comes when the European Soccer Champions League reaches the direct elimination stages, and France's SuperBowl is the Cup final in May. But the entire country eagerly awaits a bunch of other events.

The French Pro Soccer League
Le Championnat de France de Ligue 1
From August to May, 20 teams play each other twice (home and away). They get 3 points for a win, 1 for a tie, and nothing for a loss. (No penalty kick shoot-outs are allowed, except in finals and the French Open Cup.) At season's end, the last three teams drop in disgrace down into the minor league and are replaced by the top three from the second division ("Ligue 2"). Because France imposes a luxury tax, stars like Paul Pogba, Antoine Griezmann, and Franck Ribéry leave to play in the English, Italian, Spanish, or German leagues.

World Cup Soccer
La Coupe du Monde de football

It's *the* most-watched event on the planet. Americans think it's boring, but people in Brazil jump out of windows when the national team loses. Brazil has won the most titles (five), while France won it twice— in 1998 and 2018. In 2006 France lost in the finals to Italy in overtime after French superstar Zinédine Zidane was ejected from the game (the last of his career) for headbutting Italian defender Marco Materazzi for calling his sister a whore (see Chapter 6). It was a shocking end to an otherwise stellar career.

The Olympic Games (The Games)
Les Jeux Olympiques (Les J.O.)
If you catch the Olympics on French TV, a couple of things jump out at you. They actually spend most of the time televising events instead of getting "up close and personal" with the guy's crippled mother or showing you how they make cheese from goat's milk in Kazakhstan. You'll also notice they have live coverage of lesser-known sports like kayaking *(le canoë kayak)* or fencing *(l'escrime)*—probably because those are the only sports in which France has a good chance to medal.

The Tour de France
Le Tour de France

The most famous bicycle race in the world takes place every year during the first three weeks in July and covers more than 1,800 miles. Throughout the 1980s and '90s, the success of Americans Greg LeMond (three-time winner) and Lance Armstrong put cycling on the U.S. map. However, the reputation of the famed *maillot jaune* (the yellow jersey that the leader wears) has been severely damaged by doping scandals (*les scandales de dopage*), including scandals involving Lance Armstrong. Armstrong was stripped of his seven Tour de France victories in 2012, after he was charged and convicted of using performance-enhancing drugs throughout his cycling career. These guys were more juiced up than José Canseco!

The Six Nations Tournament & the Rugby World Cup
Le Tournoi des Six Nations & La Coupe du Monde de Rugby

These are the two most prestigious international rugby competitions. The Six Nations is the oldest, and only France, England, Ireland, Italy, Scotland, and Wales compete. A rugby match is played in two halves, but the rugby players are especially famous for the "third half" *(la troisième mi-temps)*: the heavy partying in bars that traditionally follows the game.

The French Open (Roland Garros)
Les Internationaux de France de Roland Garros

One of the four Grand Slam events in tennis, the French Open is played in Paris on clay in the spring. The arena is named after Roland Garros, an early French aviator who had nothing to do with tennis. But then again, the main Paris airport is named after Charles de Gaulle, a French president who had nothing to do with aviation.

The French Grand Prix & Le Mans
Le Grand Prix de France de Formule 1 & Les 24 heures du Mans

The Formula One French Grand Prix takes place every summer in Nevers Magny-Cours, 150 miles south of Paris, and features the fastest cars and best drivers in the world. At Le Mans, two drivers relay each other on the track for 24 hours straight. It was here in 1967 that a couple of Americans, Dan Gurney and A. J. Foyt, started the tradition of spraying Champagne after a race win. Although technically not held in France, the Monte Carlo Grand Prix on the French Riviera is another amazing race to watch because it takes place right in the middle of the city.

CHAPTER 9

Food & Coffee
À manger & à boire

When you're traveling, few things are more important for world peace than keeping everybody's tummy happy. Just like science could probably prove a high correlation of hunger and road rage among U.S. drivers, many a Eurotrip has crashed and burned simply due to a failure to properly appreciate the urgency of everyone's food needs. The following terms might improve your chances of not committing any acts that have permanent consequences.

Hunger
La faim

I'm starving.
J'ai la dalle.

I'm dying of hunger/of thirst.
Je crève de faim/de soif.

I could eat a horse.
J'ai les crocs.
Crocs are fangs, so it means, "I'm so hungry I grew fangs."

Let's get some....
Allons chercher de....

food
la nourriture

grub, eats
la bouffe

junk food
la malbouffe

fast food
la restauration rapide; le fast food

I'm goin' home to grab dinner.
Je rentre grailler.

Come on over, we're gonna eat some grub.
Viens, on va casser la croûte.
Literally, "to break the crust," but the phrase isn't outdated like "breaking bread."

Yum! That was....
Miam! C'était....

> **a good meal**
> *un bon repas*
>
> **really tasty**
> *vraiment réussi*
>
> **delicious**
> *délicieux*
>
> **scrumptious**
> *un régal*
>
> **filling**
> *bien assez*
> When you've had enough to eat, don't say, *Je suis plein(e)*—for French people, "I'm full" means you're preggers. So if you've hit your stopping point and need to refuse that piece of super-rich chocolate cake, simply offer up a royal, *J'ai bien mangé* (I have eaten well).

I'm about to bust a gut.
Je me suis cassé le ventre.

I'm stuffed to the gills.
J'ai les dents du fond qui baignent.
Literally, "The food has backed up to my molars."

Yum-yum!
Miam miam!

It's really good!
C'est super bon!

Yuck!
Beurk!

Their food is crap.
Ils te font manger de la merde.

It's disgusting.
C'est dégueulasse.

I'm not gonna eat this....
Je vais pas bouffer....

> **shit**
> *cette saloperie*
>
> **garbage**
> *cette pourriture*
>
> **gooey thing**
> *cette chose gluante*
>
> **ungodly thing**
> *cette chose immonde*

At the restaurant
Au restaurant/Au restau

In France, even ordering water at a restaurant can be a trip through a minefield. Your waiter, possibly a smarmy, mustachioed dude who pretends not to understand your slight accent, will ask you to specify whether you want regular water (*l'eau*), mineral water (*l'eau minérale*), or mineral water without bubbles (*l'eau minérale plate*). Respond with equal disdain by saying, "Whatever's cheap and wet" (*Donnez-moi du liquide pas cher*). Then start pounding the table and chanting, "USA! USA! USA!" They love it when you do that.

Bring me....
Apportez-moi....

> **the menu**
> *la carte*
>
> **bread**
> *du pain*
>
> **silverware**
> *des couverts*
>
> **a napkin**
> *une serviette*
>
> **the check**
> *l'addition*

Can we **order**?
*On peut **commander**?*

What do **you recommend**?
*Qu'est-ce que **vous recommandez**?*

Do I look like I wanna eat **frog legs**?
*J'ai une tête de mangeur de **cuisses de grenouilles**?*

Five bucks says you won't finish those **snails**.
*Je te parie cinq euros que tu termines pas ces **escargots**.*

What's taking so long? Did they have to **head out to the farm to find my chicken,** or what?
*Oh, mais c'est bien long! Ils sont allés **le chercher à la ferme mon poulet**, ou quoi?*

There's a fly in my soup. Call....
Il y a une mouche dans ma soupe. Appelez-moi....

DINING OUT
MANGER DEHORS

- The French eat late. Most restaurants open for dinner at 7:30 p.m.
- All-you-can-eat buffets are almost nonexistent in France. Why? Because the French would starve the entire family for two days, then show up and stuff their pockets.
- There's no bread plate; you put your bread directly on the table.
- You have to ask for the check or they won't bring it to you.

the manager
le patron

the chef
le chef

the cook
le cuistot

the waiter/the waitress
le serveur/la serveuse

the wine steward
le sommelier

the parking valet
le valet de parking
Valet is a French word...so, of course, the practice doesn't really exist in France.

If you are sitting outside (on *la terrasse*) at a nice café and want to get the server's attention, we strongly recommend:

Please, Sir/Madam
Monsieur/Madame, s'il vous plaît!

If you want them to know that you're an American traveling in France for the first time and you'd like crappy, maddeningly slow service, we strongly recommend:

Boy!/Dude!
Garçon!

Hey, get your fat ass over here!
Ho, tu te ramènes avec ton gros cul?

I don't have any dough on me, but I could **do the dishes** to settle up.
J'ai pas d'argent mais je peux faire la vaisselle pour régler la note.

....

French cuisine
La cuisine française

The same way that a hamburger with fries is the ultimate American dish, the *steak frites* (steak with fries) is the ol' standby in France. Yet to the French, fries are considered Belgian. In fact, it's common to hear Belgians called "fry eaters" (*mangeurs de frites*). In addition to this national dish, France has a variety of regional specialties.

THE NORTHWEST
LE NORD-OUEST
Yo, can I get some...?
Ho, je peux avoir...?

> ### *les moules frites*
> A big bowl of steaming, fragrant mussels accompanied by piping-hot fries.
>
> ### *la coquille Saint-Jacques*
> Scallops cooked in butter with onions and shallots, topped with grated cheese.
>
> ### *des huîtres*
> Oysters
>
> ### *les crêpes*
> Crepes; You can have them for lunch, topped with cheese, ham, and eggs, or as dessert, covered in chocolate, Nutella, sugar, or jam.

de la tarte Tatin
The French version of apple pie, served upside down and caramelized.

les bêtises de Cambrai
Delicious mint candies.

les macarons
Miniature cakes made with almonds and frosting.

la crème Chantilly
Whipped cream with a fancy name.

THE EAST
L'EST

You gotta try ....
Tu devrais essayer....

la choucroute
In the Alsace-Lorraine region, a big plate of sauerkraut comes with hot dogs (*saucisses de Francfort*), a slice of ham (*jambon*), and steamed potatoes.

l'andouillette
Chitlins, or, for those of you not from the South, pig intestines; fittingly, andouille is also slang for "dumbass."

le boudin
Blood sausage. Also slang for a very ugly person.

la quiche lorraine
There are different kinds; the famous Lorraine quiche is ham and cheese.

a flammekueche
A wood-oven baked Alsatian spin on pizza with base toppings such as cubed bacon, onions, and sour cream.

le bœuf bourguignon
A classic French stew of cubed beef slow-cooked in red wine and broth.

la fondue bourguignonne
A beef fondue in which tender, thin-sliced beef is cooked in butter and oil and dipped in flavorful sauces.

les escargots de Bourgogne
A French delicacy: cooked snails slurped down with lots of butter and parsley—dee-lish.

PROVENCE AND RIVIERA
LA PROVENCE ET LA CÔTE D'AZUR
This place makes a mean....
Ici ils font....

une super salade niçoise
A classic salad served with fresh veggies, boiled egg, tuna, anchovies, and olive oil.

une bouillabaisse magnifique
Like a French gumbo, with fish, potatoes, and soup.

HOW DO YOU WANT THAT COOKED?
POUR LA CUISSON?

In France, you can get your meat served either bleeding or burnt. There's little in between. In fact, the French don't even have words for medium or medium-rare. Most French opt for rare (a *lot* rarer than what Americans go for), partly because French meat is so tender, thanks to seasoned butchers who have mastered the technique of cutting with the grain.

Very rare
Bleu
Literally, "blue."

Rare
Saignant
Literally, "bleeding."

Medium-well
À point

Well-done
Bien cuit

Burnt to a crisp
Carbonisé

I'm a vegetarian.
Je suis végétarien(ne).

de la très bonne daube provençale
Red wine–marinated beef, cut in strips and served with pasta.

une vraie bonne tapenade
Green- or black-olive paste, for appetizers or mixed into pasta dishes.

des chichis croustillants
Made famous by an ocean-front quarter on the edge of Marseille known as l'Estaque, these sugar-coated beignets are midway between Mexico's churros and New Orleans' Café du Monde beignets.

de bons calissons
Candied almonds sweetened with crystallized cantaloupe.

CORSICA
LA CORSE
Don't leave without tasting the....
Ne partez pas sans avoir goûté....

le figatelli
Pork-liver sausage served hot and dripping with delicious fat and garlic.

le fromage corse
Incredibly stinky Corsican cheese made from goat's and sheep's milk.

le saucisson d'âne
Dried, smoked donkey sausage, which looks as appetizing as it sounds, but when done right, beats American jerky any day.

SOUTHWEST
LE SUD-OUEST
What! You've never had...?
Quoi! tu n'as jamais mangé de...?

Roquefort

A strong blue cheese aged deep in the crevices of remote mountain caves (we're not making that up—it's required by European Union regulations).

cassoulet
A perfect winter dish made with duck, sausage, goose fat, and beans; sop up the drippings with crusty bread.

THE ALPS
LES ALPES
I'm gonna go into a food coma if I eat any more....
Je vais tomber dans le coma si je reprends encore....

de la fondue savoyarde
Cheese fondue; A traditional dish, originally from Switzerland—you dip small pieces of bread into a crock with thick melted Swiss cheese (*fondre* means "to melt"); great after skiing.

du gratin dauphinois
Gratin-style potatoes with sour cream and oven-melted cheese.

de la raclette
A miniature Bunsen burner–like apparatus is used to melt raclette cheese, which will be topped with cold cuts to produce a (slightly) lighter version of fondue.

de la tartiflette
Another gratin-style potato dish, this time using cubed bacon and Reblochon cheese, and eaten in the winter months when you need to put some fat on your bones.

Cuttin' the cheese
Tranches de fromage

France has more varieties of cheese than any other country. Much like wine, every region in France has its own type. They come in all shapes, forms, colors, and smells, from the neutral, don't-offend-anybody kinds to those that smell worse than sweaty animals having sex in a barnyard. Due to recent E.U. regulations and U.S. import restrictions concerning non-pasteurized milk products, you now have to head out into the French countryside to try out some of the wildest ones.

Pass the....
Passe-moi le....

Cut me some....
Coupe-moi un morceau de....

Damn, that...smells funky.
Putain, ce....sent putain de drôle.

Brie
A mild, creamy and universally popular cow's milk cheese.

Camembert
Also from cow's milk, only slightly stronger than Brie.

Gruyère
Basically Swiss cheese, only way better than that crap you're used to getting from the "sandwich artists" at Subway; it's made from goat's milk, is dense and sharp, and comes in small servings.

Bleu d'Auvergne
From the center region of France called Auvergne, a smoother type of blue cheese.

Saint-Nectaire
Another classic from Auvergne; the most commonly produced farmer cheese in France.

(la) Mimolette

Made in the north of France near the Belgian border; cow's milk cheese whose taste and orange color make it similar to U.S. cheddars.

Boursin

Famous soft cheese from Normandy, with a pepper touch, that reached stardom with a successful worldwide TV campaign that went, *Du pain, du vin, du Boursin* (bread, wine, Boursin).

(la) Tomme de Chèvre

As the name indicates, a goat milk cheese from the Savoie region: small, rounded, hard, and tasty

Are those **worms** in that cheese?
*C'est **des vers** là dans ce fromage?*

You don't eat the **crust** on that one.
*La **peau** ne se mange pas sur celui-là.*

That cheese **stinks** like dirty socks!
*Il **sent** trop les pieds ce fromage!*

Damn, that cheese is **seriously nasty**!
*Putain comme il **shlingue** ce fromage!*

....

Coffee
Le café

Just so you know: In certain working class regions (mining towns, factory districts, etc.), if you ask for a coffee at 7 a.m., you could find yourself sitting in front of a glass of white wine or a shot of brandy. It's a custom from bygone times intended to fight against the morning chill before shuffling off to work. Another version of this tradition is a sort of coffee chaser: a shot of spirits is poured into your empty espresso cup so that it mixes with the remaining bit of coffee grounds. Guaranteed to jump-start your pacemaker.

An espresso
Un express

A double espresso
Un double

An espresso with a drop of cream
Une noisette

Coffee diluted with extra water
Un café allongé; un café américain

An American coffee with milk
Un café au lait

Every time I drink coffee, it makes me want to take a shit.
A chaque fois que je bois du café, ça me donne envie de chier.

The ABC's of sandwiches
Le B-A BA du sandwich

Except for the Bagnat and the Club, which come on hamburger buns and sliced bread, all French sandwiches are made with baguettes. While there are places called *sandwicheries* (can you guess what they serve?), you can get a sandwich almost anywhere food is sold.

I need a...sandwich.
Il me faut un sandwich au....

> **ham**
> *jambon*
>
> **ham and butter**
> *jambon-beurre*
>
> **ham and cheese**
> *jambon-fromage*
>
> **salami**
> *saucisson*
>
> **paté**
> *pâté*

cheese
fromage

I'd kill for a...
Je tuerais pour un....

pan bagnat
A deliciously slimy, stinky concoction of anchovies, tomatoes, black olives, olive oil, and onions served on a hamburger bun in Nice and Provence.

parisien
Ham, lettuce, butter: the original version of Parisian "fast food."

merguez frites
This spicy lamb sandwich stuffed with fries is the classic three-in-the-morning, drunk-and-still-partyin'-hard, fast food meal of choice for most French. It's also the sporting event equivalent of the American ballpark hot dog. Watch out for the harissa sauce on the *merguez*—it'll light your ass on fire!

croque-monsieur
The king of French sandwiches. It's basically just a grilled ham and cheese sandwich, but you have to eat it with a fork because the whole thing comes smothered in melted Gruyère cheese.

croque-madame
Same as a *croque-monsieur*, but with a fried egg.

Hey! **Easy on the** harissa!
*Oh! **Doucement avec la** harissa!*

I'd give my own life for **a hot dog**.
*Je donnerais ma vie pour **un hot-dog**.*

Never translate "hot dog" literally *(un chien chaud)*, or the counter guy will either look at you as if you just crapped on his floor or will serve you somebody's pet.

This is one **dry, boring-ass sandwich**.
*Celui-ci est un vrai **sandwich au pain**.*

If your sandwich is too dry and there's not much of anything in it, you just call that shit a "bread sandwich."

....

Food spots
Points bouffe

French restaurants aren't all white tablecloths and accordions, pricey Michelin stars, and four-hour meals. For travelers on a budget or just wanting food on the go, there's now a whole range of affordable, quick options.

Mickey D's
MacDo

Pulp Fiction stole our thunder and already taught you that French McDonald's serve beer, and that a quarter-pounder is called a *royale with cheese*. But it didn't teach you that French farmers, none too happy about processed meat, hate Mickey D's so much that every once in a while they try to bulldoze them. They even bombed a McDonald's in Millau, France's equivalent of the Midwest!

> **You wanna hit up** Mickey D's tonight?
> ***On se fait** un MacDo ce soir?*

>> To **get some grub** or to **bomb it**?
>> *Pour **aller chercher à bouffer** ou pour **le faire sauter**?*

Quick

The French fast food competitor to McDonald's. French fast food restaurants *do not* have automatic refills on drinks. (It'd kinda be a problem with the beer.)

Brasseries chez Clément

Good for traditional French meals and wine.

Pizza Païcs/Pizza del Arte

Most French pizza comes thin à la New York–style. In the south of France, you'll find pizza trucks (*camion pizza*) that cruise through the neighborhood during the week or when there are major sporting events. They actually have wood-burning ovens and make it fresh.

Buffalo Grill

A bad pun on "Buffalo Bill." Vegetarians and people who can't stand kids should sit it out in the car.

La Cafétéria (Flunch, Casino)

Cafeterias in France are self-service restaurants. Picture those American chains like Denny's that cater to the blue-hair crowd, and you're on the right track. Proof that the French *can* prepare bad food. Grab your tray and go...somewhere else?

La Taverne de Maître Kanter

A brasserie-style chain specializing in sauerkraut and beer. Mmmm... sauerkraut and beer.

Léon de Bruxelles

The *moules frites* (mussels and fries) specialists. Dip your fries in the mussel juice at the bottom of the bowl for a bit of gustatory heaven.

La Brioche Dorée

A good pastry chain to snag breakfast or lunch on the fly (they also serve salads and sandwiches). Try their *tartelette aux framboises* (raspberry tart) or a slice of their flan. You won't go wrong.

Hippopotamus

A chain of French steak houses recognizable by its hippopotamus logo. It's a restaurant rarity in France: service is non-stop from 11 a.m. to 1 a.m., seven days a week. But they don't actually serve a hippo rib eye.

About the Authors

Adrien Clautrier is a self-employed mechanic born and raised in Marseille, France. A motorcycle and car aficionado, he has completed two U.S. coast-to-coast trips, one on a Harley Davidson and the other in a Cadillac.

Henry Rowe left Berkeley, California, to play amateur soccer in France, and stayed for the used bookstores and St-Émilion wine cellars.

9 781646 043934